Global Financial Regulation

The essential guide

Howard Davies and
David Green

polity

First published in 2008 by Polity Press

Polity Press
65 Bridge Street
Cambridge CB2 1UR, UK.

Polity Press
350 Main Street
Malden, MA 02148, USA

ISBN-13: 978-07456-4349-6
ISBN-13: 978-07456-4350-2 (pb)

A catalogue record for this book is available from the British Library.

Typeset in 11 on 14pt Sabon
by Servis Filmsetting Ltd, Manchester
Printed and bound in Great Britain by MPG Books Ltd, Bodmin, Cornwall

The publisher has used its best endeavours to ensure that the URLs for
external websites referred to in this book are correct and active at the time
of going to press. However, the publisher has no responsibility for the
websites and can make no guarantee that a site will remain live or that the
content is or will remain appropriate.

Every effort has been made to trace all copyright holders, but if any have
been inadvertently overlooked the publishers will be pleased to include any
necessary credits in any subsequent reprint or edition.

For further information on Polity, visit our website: www.polity.co.uk

Contents

Acknowledgements

This modest volume is not the product of great original research but draws on the personal experience and knowledge accumulated during the time we spent as central bankers and then regulators, first within the long-established tradition of the Bank of England, and then engaged in the creation of the Financial Services Authority. The sources to which we refer are not comprehensive but those we have come across in the course of our day-to-day work and which struck us as useful and illuminating. Most of all, though, we have gained insights from the close collaboration and debate over the years with our fellow colleagues in the Bank and the FSA, some of whom agreed to review what we had written, whether in whole or in part.

We would particularly like to express our indebtedness to Paul Boyle, Alastair Clark and Paul Wright, each of whom reviewed an earlier draft in full, as well as to Ged Fitzpatrick, Piers Haben, Alan Houmann, Peter Parker and John Sloan, the last of whom devised the

Acknowledgements

forerunners to the charts we provide to help unravel the spaghetti of international committees. We are also grateful to our support staff, without whose endless patience in deciphering manuscript scribbles or making and remaking amendments, this would have never been finalized. We would particularly mention Rachel Gibson, Carol Liuzzi, Clare Taylor Gold and Tamlyn Whittock.

Lastly, as is customary, but also necessary, we need to note that the views expressed here are entirely our own and not those of any of the organizations with which we have been associated.

Abbreviations

ACAM	Autorité de Contrôle des Assurances et des Mutuelles (France)
AMF	Autorité des Marchés Financiers (France)
APRA	Australian Prudential Regulatory Authority
ASIC	Australian Securities and Investments Commission
AuRC	Audit Regulatory Committee (EU)
BAC	Banking Advisory Committee (EU)
BAKred	Bundesaufsichtsamt für das Kreditwesen (Germany)
BaFin	Bundesanstalt für Finanzdienstleistungsaufsicht (Germany)
BAV	Bundesaufsichtsamt für Versicherungswesen (Germany)
BAWe	Bundesaufsichtsamt für den Wertpapierhandel (Germany)
BCCI	Bank of Credit and Commerce International

Abbreviations

BCBS	Basel Committee on Banking Supervision
BIS	Bank for International Settlements
BOBS	Board of Banking Supervision (UK)
BOJ	Bank of Japan
BSC	Banking Supervision Committee (ECB)
BSC	Building Societies Commission (UK)
Buba	Deutsche Bundesbank
CBRC	China Banking Regulatory Commission
CCA	Commission de Contrôle des Assurances (France)
CDIC	Canada Deposit Insurance Corporation
CDO	Collateralized Debt Obligation
CEBS	Committee of European Banking Supervisors
CECEI	Comité des Établissements de Crédit et des Enterprises d'Investissement (France)
CEIOPS	Committee of European Insurance and Occupational Pensions Supervisors
CESR	Committee of European Securities Regulators
CFTC	Commodity Futures Trading Commission (US)
CIRC	China Insurance Regulatory Commission
CMF	Conseil des Marchés Financiers (France)
COB	Commission des Opérations de Bourse (France)
CONSOB	Commissione per le Società e la Borsa (Italy)
CPSS	Committee on Payment and Settlement Systems
CRD	Capital Requirements Directive

Abbreviations

CSE	Consolidated Supervised Entity (US)
CSRC	China Securities Regulatory Commission
DBERR	Department of Business, Enterprise and Regulatory Reform
DICJ	Deposit Insurance Corporation of Japan
DTI	Department of Trade and Industry (UK)
EBC	European Banking Committee
ECB	European Central Bank
EFC	Economic and Financial Committee (EU)
EFR	European Financial Services Round Table
EFRAG	European Financial Reporting Advisory Group
EGAOB	European Group of Audit Oversight Bodies
EIOPC	European Insurance and Occupational Pensions Committee
ESC	European Securities Committee
EP	European Parliament
FASB	Financial Accounting Standards Board
FATF	Financial Action Task Force
FDIC	Federal Deposit Insurance Corporation (US)
FESCO	Forum of European Securities Commissions
FGD	Financial Groups Directive
FIBV	Fédération Internationale des Bourses de Valeurs
FRC	Financial Reporting Council (UK)
FSA	Financial Services Authority (UK)
FSA	Financial Services Agency (Japan – also JFSA)

Abbreviations

FSAP	Financial Services Action Plan (EU)
FSAP	Financial Sector Assessment Programme (IMF)
FSC	Financial Services Committee (EU)
FSCS	Financial Services Compensation Scheme (UK)
FSF	Financial Stability Forum
FTA	Free Trade Agreement
GAAP	Generally Accepted Accounting Principles
GAO	Government Accountability Office (US)
GATS	General Agreement on Trade in Services
IAA	International Actuarial Association
IAASB	International Auditing and Assurance Standards Board
IADI	International Association of Deposit Insurers
IAIS	International Association of Insurance Supervisors
IAS	International Accounting Standards
IASC	International Accounting Standards Committee
IFAC	International Federation of Accountants
IFI	International Financial Institution
IFIAR	International Forum of Independent Audit Regulators
IFRS	International Financial Reporting Standards
IFSB	Islamic Financial Services Board
IIF	Institute of International Finance
IMF	International Monetary Fund
IMFC	International Monetary and Financial Committee

Abbreviations

IMRO	Investment Management Regulatory Organization (UK)
IORP	Institutions for Occupational Retirement Provision (EU)
IOSCO	International Organization of Securities Commissions
IOPS	International Organization of Pension Supervisors
IPO	Initial Public Offering
ISAs	International Standards on Auditing
ISP	Insurance Supervisory Principles
ISVAP	Istituto per la Vigilanza sulle Assicurazioni Private e di Interesse Colletivo (Italy)
JFSA	Japan Financial Services Agency
LZB	Landeszentralbanken (Germany)
LIFFE	London International Financial Futures Exchange
MiFID	Markets in Financial Instruments Directive
NAIC	National Association of Insurance Commissioners (US)
NASD	National Association of Securities Dealers (US)
NGO	Non-Governmental Organization
NRSRO	Nationally Recognized Statistical Rating Organization (US)
OCC	Office of the Comptroller of the Currency (US)
OECD	Organization for Economic Co-operation and Development
OFC	Offshore Financial Centre

Abbreviations

OPRA	Occupational Pensions Regulatory Authority (UK)
OSFI	Office of the Superintendent of Financial Institutions (Canada)
OTS	Office of Thrift Supervision (US)
PBOC	Peoples Bank of China
PCAOB	Public Company Accounting Oversight Board (US)
PIA	Personal Investment Authority (UK)
PIOB	Public Interest Oversight Board
PSD	Payment Services Directive
RFS	Registry of Friendly Societies (UK)
ROSC	Report on the Observance of Standards and Codes (IMF)
SEC	Securities and Exchange Commission (US)
SESC	Securities and Exchange Surveillance Commission (Japan)
SEPA	Single European Payments Area
SI	Systematic Internalizer
SIB	Securities and Investments Board (UK)
SRO	Self-Regulatory Organization
UCITS	Undertakings for Collective Investments in Transferable Securities (EU)
WFE	World Federation of Exchanges
WTO	World Trade Organization

Introduction

This book describes the existing system of international financial regulation and proposes some needed improvements. It assumes in the reader a certain basic knowledge of finance but it does not delve into any one subject in great technical detail; it is therefore not a complete handbook for the trader, compliance officer or line supervisor. It does not say all that can be said about current issues in the main financial disciplines, banking, securities and insurance, nor about the numerous questions needing to be addressed in the structure of regulation in the EU (and indeed elsewhere); rather it offers a bird's eye view of the main issues at the time of writing (September 2007) and gives the authors' views as to the broad direction in which solutions are to be found.

We seek to expose the remarkable range of financial regulation topics being addressed across the globe and describe the complex bureaucratic organisms through which they are discussed and occasionally resolved. These organisms have displayed a tendency to spawn.

Introduction

During the half a dozen years in which the authors were actively engaged in this field at the FSA in the UK, the number of international committees of which the FSA was a member multiplied from 76 to over 150. It is beyond the scope of this book to describe the role and composition of every one of them, though it provides links to enable the assiduous reader to drill down further. In any case, these committees constantly divide, dissolve and re-form so that no account will remain wholly reliable for long.

In Chapter 1 we remind the reader of the underlying rationale for the different kinds of financial regulation and why there is an international dimension to such activity. The financial system is in a constant state of evolution so that there is an equally constant debate about what should be regulated and what should not.

We go on in Chapter 2 to set out the main institutional arrangements for international co-operation by discipline – banking, securities, insurance and financial reporting – including some history as to how the arrangements have evolved. Chapter 3 discusses the role of the International Financial Institutions: principally the IMF and the World Bank. We then describe the much more highly developed structures for cross-border financial regulation created within the EU in Chapter 4.

Chapter 5 looks at the very diverse arrangements for the organization of supervision in the G7 countries and describes the various different philosophies underlying those structures. There is a lively debate under way in many countries about how best to respond to changing financial markets. Chapter 6 offers a brief guide to that debate. Finally, in Chapter 7, we look at the main current issues which pose a challenge to the existing arrangements and propose a number of important reforms.

The underlying argument we advance is that the international regulatory system has developed in a piecemeal fashion. It has been reasonably successful in maintaining financial stability in a fast changing world. But it is now seriously out of date and may not be adequate to address the challenges such change will bring. The global committees, whose structure is rooted in an old-fashioned breakdown of financial activity into the three 'sectors' of banking, insurance and securities, need radical reform if they are to keep pace with the rapid evolution of financial markets. The market turmoil of the summer of 2007, originating in the US sub-prime mortgage market, demonstrated vividly that the technology of credit transfer had developed to the point where it is often hard to determine where risks now lie – and it is quite impossible for the regulator of a single sector to do so.

The scale of financial market activities has escalated dramatically in recent years. McKinsey and Company estimate that global financial assets have more than doubled in the last ten years, and are set to increase by a further 50 per cent by the end of this decade (Chart 1). It is therefore not surprising that a regulatory system designed some time ago is beginning to creak. Furthermore, the growth of cross-border financial activity is even more rapid: international capital flows have been expanding at over 10 per cent a year over the last fifteen years (Chart 2). So the international

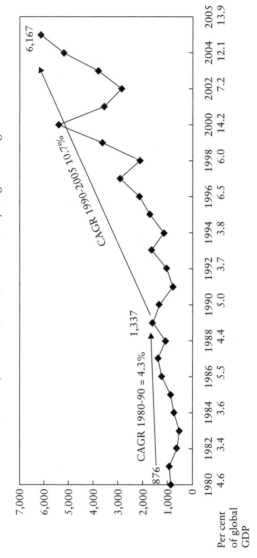

Chart 1   Total Cross-Border Capital Flows
$ billion, 2005 constant $ and constant foreign exchange

	1980	1982	1984	1986	1988	1990	1992	1994	1996	1998	2000	2002	2004	2005
Per cent of global GDP	4.6	3.4	3.6	5.5	4.4	5.0	3.7	3.8	6.5	6.0	14.2	7.2	12.1	13.9

6,167

CAGR 1990-2005 10.7%

CAGR 1980-90 = 4.3%

1,337

876

Source: McKinsey Global Institute Capital Flows Database

Chart 2   Global Financial Assets

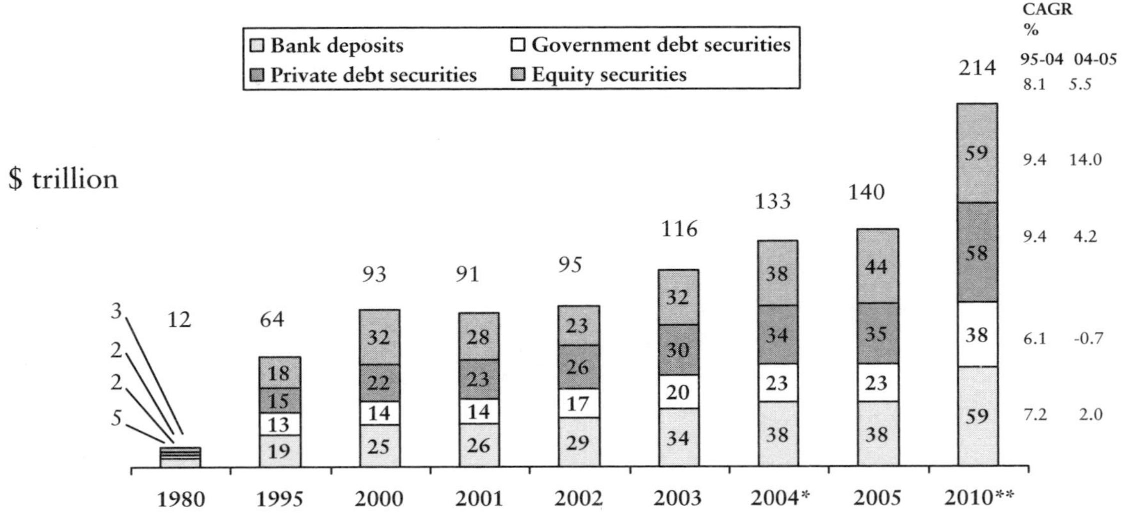

$ trillion

Legend:
- ☐ Bank deposits
- ■ Private debt securities
- ☐ Government debt securities
- ■ Equity securities

	1980	1995	2000	2001	2002	2003	2004*	2005	2010**	CAGR % 95-04	04-05
Total	12	64	93	91	95	116	133	140	214	8.1	5.5
Equity securities		18	32	28	23	32	38	44	59	9.4	14.0
Private debt securities		15	22	23	26	30	34	35	58	9.4	4.2
Government debt securities		13	14	14	17	20	23	23	38	6.1	-0.7
Bank deposits		19	25	26	29	34	38	38	59	7.2	2.0
1980 components	3, 2, 2, 5										

	1980	1995	2000	2001	2002	2003	2004*	2005	2010**		7.5
Nominal GDP $ trillion	10.1	29.4	31.7	31.6	32.8	36.9	41.4	44.5	63.3	4.2	7.5
Depth (FS/GDP), %	109	218	292	289	290	315	322	316	338		

* 2004 figure dropped from $136 trillion to $133 trillion due to restatement of data by individual countries

** Extrapolation off 2005 base, with components grown at 2000-5 CAGRs

Source: McKinsey Global Institute Global Financial Stock Database

dimension of financial regulation is no longer a marginal add-on to the domestic regime, as it has long been seen in the US; it is the central question in financial markets today.

1

The Objectives of International Financial Regulation

At the beginning of the twenty-first century financial markets are more international than ever before. Capital markets were highly integrated before the First World War, with massive flows of funds from developed to developing countries, but the degree of integration fell sharply during the next fifty years and capital movements were often highly controlled. Now, however, 'globalized capital markets are back, but with a difference: capital transactions seem to be mostly a rich–rich affair, a process of diversification finance rather than development finance'.[1] It is not true to say, as some do, that we live in a borderless world, but finance certainly flows more easily across borders than do goods or services.

The channels of financial intermediation have also changed. While only twenty years ago most business flowed through the balance sheets of banks or insurance companies, or through a limited range of investment funds usually dealing in products traded on regulated markets, the explosive increase in wealth held privately (partly as a result of greater dispersion of income) has led to the creation of a wide range of other investment vehicles, of which hedge funds and private equity are the most prominent, funded by high net worth investors and organized on an informal, largely unregulated basis.

New instruments have emerged which make it possible to transfer risk of all kinds on a far larger scale and in more complex ways, not solely through standardized exchange-traded derivatives, but through an almost infinite range of bespoke, over-the-counter arrangements: CDOs, synthetic CDOs and the like. In some cases banks hold them in off-balance sheet vehicles. While these instruments make it possible to lay off risk over a vastly greater range of risk bearers, which probably increases the system's resilience, they also mean that when risks crystallize they may well have an impact in hitherto unfamiliar places, anywhere in the globe. They may make it easier to ride through small crises, but large ones will have many more dimensions of which we currently have no knowledge. This matters, because the last ten years or so during which these markets have evolved have also been remarkably benign in financial terms, but characterized by ready availability of credit on an unprecedented scale and consequently in some sectors by unprecedented levels of debt. Because of the structural changes which have taken place, the ways in which lenders and borrowers will react in the face of any major shock or prolonged downturn will test the financial architecture in ways for which the existing arrangements may be unprepared.

There are other new features of global capital markets. The most important is the growing dominance of a small number of huge institutions. A handful of 'bulge bracket' investment banks dominate the major markets in corporate and sovereign debt and equity, most of them headquartered in the United States. Some commercial banks like Citigroup and HSBC have built significant market shares in many countries' domestic markets. In a few large countries, such as Poland and Mexico, the majority of domestic banking is undertaken by subsidiaries of overseas institutions. The emergence of hostile cross-border bank takeovers, previously unknown, will accelerate that trend. Now even national stock exchanges, once seen as symbols of national virility, like the flag carrier airline, are owned by foreign interests. Euronext, which includes the national exchanges of France, Belgium, the Netherlands and Portugal, as well as the UK futures exchange, has been bought by the New York Stock Exchange.

A small number of marketplaces, notably New York and London, increasingly dominate transactions in both cash and derivatives markets. Technology has allowed them to take on additional business from anywhere in the globe at very low cost. That, combined with the search for speed and liquidity, and a kind of 'winner takes all' phenomenon, is driving further geographical concentration.

But as concentration in the financial industry has grown, the global economy itself has become multipolar. Economic activity is no longer dominated by the United States and Europe, but spread much more broadly, including across markets once described as emerging. Thus there have been fundamental changes in both financial architecture and in the real economy, but no alignment between the two. It is not the purpose of this book to question the welfare benefits that may or may not accrue from these developments, or to argue the case for or against free capital movement or floating exchange rates. Our focus is on the challenges these developments pose for financial regulation, and on whether the global system of financial regulation, if it can be described as a system, is adequate to handle the consequences of these growing inter-dependencies. By financial regulation we principally mean the processes of authorizing, regulating and supervising financial institutions themselves, and the traded markets within which they operate. We comment only in passing on the macro-economic dimensions of financial market oversight and on the implications for markets and economies of different tax regimes. And we say relatively little about the interaction between financial regulation and the rest of the legal system – a subject which could justify a book in itself – though we comment on some important links, such as with insolvency regimes.

Even with those important exclusions, the field is broad, and the diversity remarkable. Financial regulation encompasses a wide range of activities, from setting accounting standards, through bank capital requirements to insider dealer legislation, controls on money laundering and rules on investor protection. We traditionally think of three principal sub-sectors of finance: banking, securities and insurance, but as our analysis will show, these sectors are increasingly interlinked, and the boundaries between them increasingly blurred.

The Objectives of International Financial Regulation

The major questions we will seek to answer are:

- how well suited is the system of financial regulation to today's capital markets?
- has it kept pace with the massive growth in cross-border activity and the changed patterns of intermediation?
- are changes needed to strengthen our defences against both financial instability and market abuse?

Many would argue that the answers to these questions are clear, and that the system is obviously inadequate. The collapse of Long Term Capital Management in 1998 and the Asian financial crisis at the end of the 1990s crystallized concerns about whether the regulatory system, pieced together in an ad-hoc manner over the previous two decades, was able to address the challenges of globalization. Some argued then for the creation of a world financial authority with wide ranging powers to handle cross-border regulatory issues.[2] After some debate these calls were rejected by the G7 Finance Ministers, in favour of more modest changes, notably the establishment of the Financial Stability Forum as a co-ordinating mechanism between existing structures, and an increased focus by the IMF and the World Bank on the quality of financial regulation in member countries.

Since then further modest improvements have been made, but recent market developments have once again generated questions about their adequacy. As cross-border stock exchanges are created, how will they be overseen? Can the regulators work together effectively to supervise a consolidated system of exchanges? Have hedge funds and, more recently, private equity funds created threats to financial stability and to the integrity of traded markets which the system is not designed to address? How can the rapid growth of Islamic finance, with its rejection of the traditional concept of interest, be accommodated in a system designed well before it began to emerge as a significant market phenomenon? Specifically in the European Union, there are those who argue that a single integrated financial market, especially those parts of it with a single currency, necessarily requires a creation of a single regulator.

How powerful are these arguments? Is the regulation of the global financial system still fit for purpose, if it ever was? If it is under strain, what changes might realistically be made to improve its robustness?

It is the aim of this book to suggest answers to these questions. Before doing so, however, it is necessary to explain why we seek to regulate financial markets and financial institutions. What are the regulators trying to achieve, and what expectations can we realistically have of them?

Why regulate financial markets?

One might expect to find a simple answer to the question, but in fact this is heavily contested intellectual territory. The basic economic rationale is straight forward. There can be externalities generated by financial market activity, which are not easily capable of being addressed by private sector actors. But the prime definition of those externalities, and the nature of the interventions they justify is the subject of constant debate. Even if we exclude the extremes of the argument – those who argue for rigid state control of the financial sector, and those who prefer no regulatory interference whatsoever – there are many differences of opinion on the degree of regulation. When the British system of financial regulation was overhauled in the Financial Services and Markets Act 2000, there were lengthy debates about the intensity of intervention that should be allowed, and indeed about the borderline between statutory and self-regulation in markets. Similarly, since the passage of the Sarbanes–Oxley Act in the United States, which greatly extended the reach of regulation in the accounting and auditing field, there has been an intense debate about whether regulation has, in some sense, 'gone too far' and should be reined back. For the first time there are powerful voices in the US, including Treasury Secretary Hank Paulson, arguing that regulation is too detailed and intrusive, with damaging consequences for America's capital markets.[3] In his memoir, 'The Age of Turbulence', Alan Greenspan recommends that 'Regulation approved in a crisis must subsequently be fine-tuned', identifying the Sarbanes–Oxley Act as 'today's prime candidate for revision'.[4]

The ebb and flow of this debate is familiar. After every financial crisis there are calls for regulation to be ratcheted up. A few years later a reaction begins to emerge, as the costs become evident, and the benefits are less so. At present, the pendulum is swinging violently. Regulated firms and markets think they are over-controlled, while many politicians, by contrast, think there is too much scope to avoid regulation, and too much evidence of investor detriment and unjustified enrichment on the part of financial sector professionals. The recent sub-prime mortgage crisis in the United States, which spread to other markets, was a test case for these arguments.

There is no doubt that regulation imposes high costs on financial institutions and markets, costs which are ultimately passed through to the end user. It is also clear that 'excessive' regulation can damage the functioning of financial markets and reduce their economic utility. In any system of regulation, there is a balance to be struck between safety and soundness on the one hand and risk taking on the other. The incidence of bank and insurance company failure might be significantly reduced by tighter capital requirements, but the returns available to depositors and policy holders will be correspondingly reduced. The terms on which investments can be offered to the public can be restricted, but the opportunity to diversify into more profitable assets is also correspondingly constrained. In recent years hedge funds have, as a class, outperformed regulated collective investment schemes, yet retail investors have typically not been able to access them directly.

Against that background, it is important to have a clear understanding of the rationale for regulation, against which proposals for an expansion (or, less frequently, contraction) of the regime can be assessed. In principle, regulatory intervention should only be justified where the benefits clearly exceed the costs imposed. But cost benefit assessments of regulation are still in their infancy, in spite of much effort by the UK FSA and others. The costs are usually easier to quantify than the benefits, but the benefits appeal more to politicians. (A useful expanded discussion of the economic rationale for financial regulation can be found in Llewellyn.)[5]

Prudential standards

There are two principal strands to the rationale for regulating some financial markets, businesses and transactions.

The *first* relates to the problem of systemic risk. There is persuasive evidence that a stable financial system provides a favourable environment for efficient resource allocation and therefore promotes economic growth. However, experience shows that, left to themselves, financial systems are prone to bouts of instability and contagion. A World Bank study shows that there were 112 systemic banking crises in 93 countries between the late 1970s and the end of the twentieth century.[6] Another study by Eichengreen and Bordo argues that 'relative to the pre-1914 era of financial globalization, crises are twice as prevalent today'.[7] And the incidence of financial crisis has tended to rise as financial markets have become more liberalized and more international.

The cost of crisis does not fall only on the banks themselves, or their shareholders and depositors. In the last three decades of the last century there were 10 countries, from Mexico to Israel, where the fiscal cost of bailing out the banking system was more than 10 per cent of GDP, a cost which was borne by taxpayers. So if we can find ways of reducing the incidence of systemic crisis without excessively constraining the functionality of the markets, there is a powerful case for adopting them.

The traditional systemic risk argument for the prudential supervision of banks starts from the premise that banks, through their role in maturity transformation and the provision of liquidity, occupy a special position in the financial system. They sit at the centre of the payments network and the failure of one bank can bring about a domino effect on others. The potential externalities of such a failure cannot easily be internalized. Walter Bagehot's Lombard Street[8] remains the classic exposition of this argument. So there may be a case in certain circumstances for rescuing a failing institution in the interests of minimizing the costs which may fall on others, rather than in the interests of the bank's own depositors and shareholders.

There is often a very difficult decision to make about whether an individual bank failure is likely to be systemic or not. The Bank of England's view in relation to Barings, for example, was that it would not be, and it therefore declined to extend support. In the event Barings was bought by another bank (ING) for one pound sterling. Most people now think that the Bank of England's judgement was correct. There is also a difficult question as to whether this systemic argument now applies to other, non-banking institutions. The case of Long Term Capital Management, whose failure in 1998 did seem to threaten systemic consequences, is suggestive in this context. In the event, the New York Federal

Reserve did not provide financial support, though it convened a group of investment banks which did so. (The then President of the Fed, Bill McDonough, always maintains that the cost to the Fed was only a plate of doughnuts.)

Nonetheless, it is clear that the failure of a large investment bank, or a large insurance company, would have widespread ramifications for the financial system as a whole. The British Memorandum of Understanding between the Bank of England, the Treasury and the Financial Services Authority[9] creates a framework in which the potential systemic consequences of non-bank failures can be assessed, but it is factually the case that no bail out of a non-bank has yet been seen to be justified in the UK under the new regime, and it is hard to think of examples elsewhere, either.

But this amounts to a justification for a lender of last resort function, typically held by the central bank, to supply liquidity and conceivably solvency support, and not necessarily for the whole apparatus of prudential supervision carried out by a regulatory authority, whether a central bank or some other agency. It would be possible to operate a completely hands-off approach from year to year, meeting banks only when they run into serious trouble. So why do more, why supervise on a continuing basis?

Here there are two main arguments. The first is about externalities. In running their businesses, we may presume that bank managers and shareholders do take account of the risk of loss to themselves if their bank fails, in terms of lost jobs, lost reputation and lost shareholder value (which should never be underpinned by the lender of last resort). The Bank of England has made it explicit that in the UK the price of public support will typically be that shareholders will lose their investment and top management their jobs. But banks do not necessarily take account of the potential external cost to the economy of their failure. So they will tend to take greater risks than they would do if there was a market for this risk. Supervision aims to counteract potentially excessive risk taking by requiring banks to hold larger reserves than they might otherwise do, and to conduct their business with more careful attention to risk.

Secondly, it has to be recognized that the existence of a lender of last resort function has a cost, although in each individual case it should also be less than the cost of letting the bank in question fail. (Note that there should be a clear distinction between liquidity support to a fundamentally sound bank, which is exclusively the preserve of central banks, and solvency support which should involve finance ministries. In practice the two are often confused.) Continuing prophylactic supervision, in the form of monitoring the capital reserve position and risk management arrangements of the institution, is designed to reduce the expected cost of lender of last resort support. It should make it less likely that a bank will get into difficulties and, if it does, make it more likely that earlier remedial action can be taken.

There is a related point arising from the existence of deposit protection schemes. If it is accepted that individual retail depositors should be protected, whether wholly or substantially, from the implications of bank failure, then there is an argument for supervision to protect the Exchequer, or the private sector contributors to the deposit protection fund, if there is one, from the potential costs of such failure. Insuring depositors creates a further opportunity for an individual bank to take excess risks, in that the consequences will not be felt by the majority of its depositors, who will therefore look less closely at the creditworthiness of the bank. Once again there is an argument for supervision to offset the incentives for additional risk taking that this insurance creates.

But what kind of intervention is justified by these arguments? There is a case for capital requirements which provide a cushion against loss and increase market confidence, though care is needed to ensure that these requirements are not too large, and that they do not encourage exaggerated pro-cyclical behaviour. There is a case, too, for liquidity requirements which reduce institutions' vulnerability to shocks. These two conditions are largely uncontroversial. But, in addition, there are arguments for requiring institutions to maintain adequate management and control frameworks. That, in turn, argues for an approach based on informed judgement by supervisors, in a continuous dialogue with the firm. If one accepts the management and control arguments, then it is not possible to put prudential supervision of banks onto a purely objective, statistical basis.

These arguments are now broadly accepted by all countries which allow the operation of independent private sector banks. They are contested by some academics, and World Bank economists, who argue that it should be possible to use market discipline more effectively, perhaps through requiring each bank to issue a tranche of subordinated debt whose price would reflect market perceptions of the bank's risk management and creditworthiness and hence cause the bank to modify its behaviour.[10] A system of that kind could, it is argued, remove the need for continuous supervision. But, so far, no major country has been prepared to 'disarm' in regulatory terms and to rely on such a mechanism.

There are doubters, too, among the regulators themselves. In his recent book Alan Greenspan describes his growing scepticism about the effectiveness of prudential regulation. He says bluntly that 'Regulators can still pretend to provide oversight, but their capabilities are much diminished and declining.' And he claims that, at the Federal Reserve, he and his colleagues 'increasingly judged that we would have to rely on counterparty surveillance to do the heavy lifting'.

How do these arguments about the nature and effectiveness of prudential supervision apply to international financial regulation, which is our prime focus? If banks operated only in their country of incorporation, where their principal supervisor is located, then it would be possible to allow individual countries a considerable degree of discretion as to how they regulate their own institutions. They could set capital requirements as they wished, and be as intrusive, or hands-off as they chose in the operation of prudential supervision. But if we allow cross-border banking, and particularly if we allow banks to operate through branches, using the security of the balance sheet of the home country bank, rather than through separately capitalized subsidiaries, than it becomes essential to promote some degree of standardization of banking supervision across the world before there can be any degree of mutual reliance. Fair competition on a level playing field implies common standards. Each country needs to know that the others are adopting similar definitions of what they mean by capital, for example, and are setting capital requirements at a level which reduces the risk of failure to an acceptable and comparable minimum. The safety and soundness of a branch network in country B generally depends on the capital position in parent country A. Even separately capitalized foreign subsidiaries might very well not survive the failure of the parent.

That said, the financial position of a firm when operating as a going concern may be quite different from its value after failure. Insolvency rules are set at a national level and in particular they vary in their treatment of bank branches. Some jurisdictions are happy to leave the creditors within their jurisdiction to take their share of the value of the failed bank as a whole, known as the single entity approach, while others, pursuing the separate entity approach, freeze the assets within their jurisdiction for the benefits of local creditors. Very few multinational banks have failed, but the conflict of national insolvency requirements which emerged when BCCI collapsed drew vivid attention to this issue. Nonetheless, efforts to devise a uniform approach have never succeeded. Indeed, it could be argued that the lack of legal clarity about who will owe what to whom in the event of insolvency constitutes the largest single obstacle to the smooth management of any future international crisis. Fear of the uncertainty about who gets what when a cross-border firm collapses lies behind a number of issues to which we will return later.

Conduct of business

The second pillar of the rationale for financial regulation is the argument that there are information asymmetries in the market which a regulatory system can help to correct.

Shareholders inevitably know less about the economic circumstances of the companies in which they invest than does the management of those companies. Management has a clear incentive not to disclose bad news to the market, or only to do so after they have sold their own shares, or perhaps left the company. So there is a strong justification for rules against the abuse of insider information, and to specify the nature and timing of disclosures. In the UK firms are under a continuous obligation to disclose material information which may affect their share price. Other countries take a more periodic approach to disclosure, but the principle is the same. These rules apply to both wholesale and retail markets.

But there are additional arguments which apply where retail investors are concerned, especially when they invest through intermediaries. In the retail market the nature of the contract proposed between the firm and the individual may be difficult to understand, both in respect of what it is designed to achieve, and in relation to the inbuilt charges. Also, the performance against the terms of the contract will depend on the financial soundness of the intermediary or the investment firm, and the retail consumer does not have the expertise to judge that soundness, nor can she acquire the information to do so except at an unrealistic cost. This is a particular problem with long term financial products where the customer relies on the solvency and behaviour of the firm long after the purchase decision. Indeed the value to the customer of that solvency typically increases over time, as his ability to monitor it declines.

In principle, there could be a private sector solution to this problem in the form of rating agencies, which aim to give an independent assessment of the risk of an investment. But those agencies are typically not providing services to consumers, and find it difficult to capture from consumers the cost of their ratings service. They are paid by the institutions whose soundness they assess. So there is collective advantage in ensuring that there is a single collector and monitor of information on financial soundness. We see, therefore, a strong welfare case both for the regulation of information and transparency in savings and investment markets, and indeed for prudential supervision of firms who offer their own liabilities as assets in those markets.

Turning to the international dimension, one can again see that there is a case for some standardization across markets, albeit that the rationale is not quite as powerful as in the case of prudential supervision. Investors and shareholders will benefit from protection across borders and indeed may expect it. Otherwise firms could simply evade domestic conduct of business rules by operating through a subsidiary in a third country which sells back into their domestic markets. There is an argument, for instance, for a common definition of insider information, or for a common definition of a retail investor, as different protections typically apply in that case. Where the same shares are traded on markets in different jurisdictions, the case for a common approach to conduct of business regulation becomes stronger. And it is even more powerful in the case of a single financial market on the lines of the one under construction in the European Union, though a different political balance from the one which applies in the prudential area may be struck.

These arguments underpin the attempts to reach common agreements on various aspects of securities market regulation, which are described below.

Financial stability

Many of the justifications for regulation may now be found under the heading of maintaining or promoting financial stability. Indeed the financial stability industry has been growing so rapidly in recent years that it is surprising to note that the term itself is a relatively recent coinage. In a paper on the subject published in 2005, Allen and Wood[11] say the first use of the term was made by the Bank of England in 1994. And the Bank of England was the first institution to launch a financial stability review (in which both the present authors were engaged) in 1996. (It is now renamed the Financial Stability Report.[12] Since then, the term has become one in general and pervasive use. The IMF publish a regular global financial stability report, with many other countries, including France and China, producing their own domestic financial stability reports. And, as we have already noted, there is a Financial Stability Forum at the centre of the world's regulatory networks.

It may be surprising, therefore, that there is, according to Charles Goodhart[13] 'no good way to define, nor certainly to give a quantitative measurement of, financial stability'. And a recent review of practice around the world by Osterloo and De Haan[14] noted that there is 'no unambiguous definition of financial stability or systemic risk, and that generally the responsibility is not explicitly formulated in laws, so there is considerable heterogeneity in the way central banks pursue their financial stability objectives'.

Some have tried to define it. Mishkin argues that it is 'the prevalence of a financial system, which is able to ensure in a lasting way, and without major disruptions, an efficient allocation of savings to investment opportunities'.[15] This may seem clear, but it is extremely hard to measure, either ex-ante or ex-post. So many others have decided that it is easier to approach a definition of financial stability by defining what we mean by financial instability, or by financial crisis.

Here Allen and Wood are helpful. They define episodes of financial instability as 'episodes in which a large number of parties, whether they are households, companies or individual governments, experience financial crises which are not warranted by their previous behaviour'. They suggest that 'a distinguishing feature of episodes of financial instability is that innocent bystanders get hurt'. In the market turmoil of the summer of 2007, Northern Rock depositors clearly perceived such a risk.

As with all definitions in this area, it begs a number of questions, and depends in practice on the exercise of judgement. But in our experience regulators do use such a test in practice. They ask whether the consequences of failure, or closure of an individual institution, would be such as to damage confidence in the sector as a whole – with adverse consequences for depositors, investors or policyholders. In our view, a definition along these lines is preferable to the broader definitions of financial stability adopted by some central banks, which can be used to justify a wide range of interventions in markets. A financial stability objective is not the same as a price stability objective, where consistent low inflation is clearly a positive virtue. In markets, not all extravagant movements can or should be constrained, and not all firm failures should be seen as a failure of the regulatory regime. There may be a danger, therefore, in seeing monetary and financial stability as two sides of the same coin.

It is, nonetheless, important for financial supervisors to have regard to the interests of the financial system as a whole, or they may be led into taking individual decisions on consumer protection which can damage the system, and indeed the interests of the consumers they are seeking to protect. But they should be careful not to think, or imply, that supervisors can maintain a smooth path for asset prices, or guarantee the existence of a particular set of financial institutions indefinitely. They should be aware of the long term benefits of creative destruction.

They should also be cautious in describing the limits of their ambitions, both in terms of the degree of security they can offer to those who transact with financial institutions, and in terms of the scale or scope of the supervision they undertake. A regulator which claims too much will weaken market discipline, which can often be a more effective tool than regulatory intervention.

Those arguments are not universally accepted. Different countries, at different times, may have different tolerance for market instability and for institutional failure. Countries may also believe that they can attract mobile international business by maintaining a lax, or under-regulated environment. They may therefore be reluctant to subscribe to international norms which constrain their flexibility. Those are the underlying difficulties in reaching international agreements on financial regulation. It is to those agreements that we now turn our attention. (For a longer discussion of different approaches to Financial Stability see Davies 2006.)[16]

Regulation and competition

Governments change their minds from time to time about just how much regulation they want. Typically, informed public opinion fluctuates in cycles. There will be some kind of damaging incident which leads to demands for regulation to be tightened. Inevitably, this takes time to agree and implement. By this stage, the circumstances which led to the change in regime will have faded in the collective memory and the new rules may come to be seen as excessively bureaucratic and damaging to business efficiency. There will then be regulatory liberalization, which may very well just be being implemented when the next crisis hits. As a generality, regulation will permanently be out of alignment with public opinion.

Examples of this phenomenon can be seen in the recent histories of the US and the UK. The series of accounting scandals starting with the failure of Enron in October 2001 led to calls for a massive increase in public oversight which found legislative expression in the Sarbanes–Oxley Act. Five years later this is seen as having been damaging to the efficiency of US business and the competitiveness of US capital markets.[17] In the UK, the BCCI and Barings scandals brought into disrepute the informal, doctor-like approach of the Bank of England, criticized as over-sensitive to the needs of its clients, and to demands for a rules-based policeman to take its place. A decade later, the FSA is being pressed to move away from rules to principles, exercised by supervisors using judgement, and to rely more on codes drawn up by the industry. There are similar calls in the US.

But before moving to the detail, it is important to note that, because regulation is implemented on a national basis and because it works by limiting the free play of markets, it can also constitute a barrier to cross-border trade in financial services. Indeed, there is no doubt that in many cases regulation has been used quite deliberately as a tool to protect domestic markets from foreign incursion. For that reason, there have been efforts over the years, as part of wider efforts to dismantle barriers to trade, to include financial services within those negotiations. The latter have usually involved initiatives to include access rights for foreign institutions as part of trade negotiations, whether at the multilateral or bilateral level. However, such efforts may cut across the reasonable need to provide protections to users of financial services. It has become accepted that it is legitimate to limit free access through use of a 'prudential carve-out', that is to deny access on a case-by-case basis to individual foreign firms if they fall short of reasonable prudential standards. Attempts to define what is reasonable through the World Trade Association's (WTO) General Agreement on Trade in Services (GATS)[18] have yet to be concluded, so negotiations on opening up markets to competition, through bilateral Free Trade Agreements (FTA), continue to be pursued on a case-by-case basis. However, over the years there has been increasing agreement on what constitutes a reasonable standard, the use of which provides some objective basis for accepting or rejecting financial firms from another country on the basis of their home country regulation.

There will always be tensions between regulation and competition, as between security and risk – which is typically associated with higher returns. Those tensions will never be resolved once and for all. But we should now ask whether the current international arrangements are able to set the balance appropriately.

Better regulation

While it is not surprising that the scale and scope of financial regulation continues to expand with every effort to prevent the recurrence of a previous crisis, or to deal with the unexpected or unwelcome side effects of innovation, the cumulative effect of ever larger and more complex rule books has been to lead to calls to add financial regulations to the categories of regulation to which increasingly prominent attempts are made to apply the disciplines of what is known in the EU as 'better regulation'. These disciplines tend to be somewhat fuzzy, but the intent is to roll back rules which either fail to meet the target accurately or do so at unacceptable cost, as well as to prevent their introduction in the first place by undertaking a prior assessment of their impact.

Better regulation processes, typically involving evidence-based regulatory impact analysis, which as well as economic cost benefit analysis may also include social and environmental concerns, has been introduced under various guises with varying degrees of rigour in many national jurisdictions. Thus, in the UK, the FSA seeks to intervene only in response to identified national market failures that relate to its statutory objectives, and only when justified by cost benefit analysis, Other jurisdictions, such as the US, are required legally to accompany proposed rules with impact analysis. There has been increasing emphasis on the use of such disciplines within the EU as concerns have mounted that some parts of the Financial Services Action Plan have not delivered what they were expected to deliver or have delivered it at a disproportionate cost. Mather and Vibert set out the issues in the EU in a useful paper 'Evaluating Better Regulation: Building the System'.[19] The disciplines concerned include consultation with shareholders, consideration wherever possible of the use of non-legislative tools e.g. competition or codes of conduct, impact assessment of proposed policy options and subsequent review of measures to address their actual impact.

The European Commission is now committed to better regulation, but, as we discuss later, these disciplines are difficult to put into practice, particularly where there is a lack of clarity or agreement over the outcome legislation is intended to achieve as, for example, in the case of the slogan of 'supervisory convergence'.

Progress is now also starting to be made in developing more risk-based approaches in the decision-making processes of the international standard-setting bodies (see Chapter 2).

2

The Current International Regulatory System: Theory and Practice

It is just possible, by selecting only the most important institutions and committees, to capture the essence of the international system of financial regulation on one page. Chart 3 does so. Even this simplified map is intimidating in its complexity. In this chapter we try to explain why things are as they are before, later, proposing reforms.

Although financial markets are increasingly inter-linked, the international regulatory system operates on a sectoral basis. That is increasingly a problem, as we shall explain. But to understand the way things work today, it is still necessary to look at the different subsets of financial institutions separately.

Banking

The Basel Committee

Banking supervisors, whether formally designated as such, or in the form of central banks concerned about the

Chart 3   *Global Committee Structure – A Regulator's View*

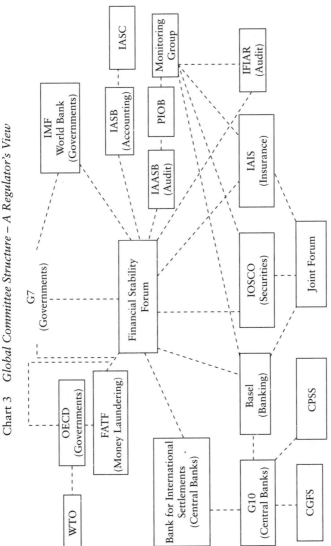

Source: Adapted with permission from Sloan and Fitzpatrick in Chapter 13, The Structure of International Market Regulation, in Financial Markets and Exchanges Law, Oxford University Press, March 2007

creditworthiness of their counterparts or about financial stability more generally, have always had an interest in international affairs. Banks have operated foreign branches since at least the fourteenth century and cross-border risks have always had a major impact on banks' soundness. Central bank governors have discussed the health of their respective banking systems in their regular meetings in Basel ever since the Bank for International Settlements (BIS) was created between the two world wars. As they created separate departments for banking supervision, or as separate banking supervisory agencies were established, it was natural that their representatives should also meet in Basel. Such discussions were inevitably informal, but, in response to events, the relationships between supervisors gradually became more formalized.

In the aftermath of serious disturbances in international currency and banking markets, and notably the failure of Bankhaus Herstatt in West Germany, the central bank governors of the Group of Ten countries decided in 1974 to establish a Committee on Banking Regulations and Supervisory Practices, subsequently renamed the Basel Committee on Banking Supervision.[1]

The precipitating factor for these more formal arrangements was the uncertainty the Herstatt affair had uncovered about which supervisor, if any, was responsible for the foreign operations of a bank, and what that responsibility entailed. The collapse of Herstatt had made it plain that there was no common understanding and led to a debate as to which supervisor was responsible in the event of liquidity and hence potentially solvency problems in

34

overseas operations. There was uncertainty as to whether the responsibility for supervision lay with the home supervisor or the host in a foreign country. This in turn created uncertainty as to where the onus lay to provide financial support in the event of collapse. Where operations were conducted through a branch rather than a legally separately constituted subsidiary, how did that affect the supervisor's responsibility?

The Committee was established under the authority of the G10 governors, most of whose central banks were at the time the banking supervisors in their jurisdiction. The membership was therefore dominated numerically by European countries and has remained so, even as the profile of the world's banking system changed. (The committee's structure, representativeness and accountability is discussed further in Chapter 7.)

The new committee set out to close gaps in the supervisory net so that no foreign banking establishment could escape supervision and that supervision should be adequate. This led to the first of the agreements made in Basel between banking supervisors, the so-called 'Concordat' of 1975, which for the first time set out some understandings on the respective responsibilities of home and host supervisors. Since then the committee's activities have entailed exchanging information on national supervisory arrangements; improving the effectiveness of techniques for supervising international banking business and, most prominently, setting minimum supervisory standards in areas where they are considered desirable. The committee has subsequently elaborated the work done in the Concordat and in particular articulated the principle of consolidated supervision of international banking groups. Such consolidated supervision necessitated tackling obstacles to the flow of prudential information between supervisors, particularly those arising out of banking secrecy regulation.

However, the topic to which the committee has devoted most time in recent years is capital adequacy. With the continuing growth in international trade and investment, the scale of the foreign operations of banks also grew rapidly and foreign firms started to account for significant market shares in the main financial centres. This immigration led to increased competition in those key marketplaces and, particularly when some groups of banks undercut on pricing, to the realization that supervisory arrangements and, in particular, capital requirements varied greatly between jurisdictions. That in turn compounded existing concerns about predatory behaviour and brought with it the fear that the collapse of under-capitalized foreign banks could cause market disruption. That fear was heightened because capital ratios appeared to be deteriorating just at the time when international risks were increasing, notably vis-à-vis heavily indebted countries.

These concerns led to debates about how to ensure that foreign banks were adequately capitalized and how to remove a source of competitive inequality arising from differences in national capital requirements. Some argued that solvency should be supervised by the host regulator of foreign branches and attempts were made in some jurisdictions to do so, without conspicuous success. The only feasible approach in the long run was for the home country supervisor to set capital requirements for the bank as a whole.

Negotiations started in the mid-1980s amongst the three countries most concerned over the issue of foreign branches: the US, the UK and Japan. The aim was to reach a common basis for measuring and setting capital, which could then be used as a basis for mutual recognition in order to allow a foreign bank into a host country marketplace without separately reviewing its capital. It was necessary to agree both a process for measuring capital and to fix what the minimum acceptable ratio might be.

The parties had mixed negotiating objectives (a feature common to most international negotiations about setting regulatory standards at the international level). Some wanted to preserve their existing domestic system to the maximum extent possible, either to minimize the potential costs of change or to preserve particular features thought to be attractive. Others recognized the need for reform in their domestic arrangements, but found it easier to pray in aid alleged foreign pressure as a means to overcome domestic opposition.

Comparing systems of supervision proved to be a complex process. There was tension between finding the best theoretical basis for judging capital and using those systems already in place in some of the major, more sophisticated centres. In the mid-1980s, the UK had just introduced a new method of measuring capital which attached risk ratios to assets, rather than simply using a gearing ratio which related capital to the overall balance sheet. In the US, a number of leading banks had individual systems to which they were particularly attached. The Japanese had their own traditional structures, which permitted double-counting of capital when banks had cross-share holdings in each other, as well as a complex system of discretionary 'administrative guidance'. And so on.

Common ground was eventually reached, involving change for all parties. A ratio was fixed as the minimum acceptable. The fact that there could be no objective basis for determining the 'right' level of capital bedevilled the negotiations. The figure of 8 per cent that was eventually chosen had no rigorous objective basis, but was judged to be the kind of level that would allow well-run banks to stay out of trouble most of the time.

Another feature which was to recur in subsequent negotiations was the need to negotiate an agreement between the biggest global marketplaces and for that to be accepted, both technically and politically, within the EU, with its broad range of disparate national banking structures ranging from complex international banks to small rural savings banks. This was important because, while the Accord finally reached applied formally only to internationally active banks, within the EU there was at least a presumption that any standard should apply to all banks, irrespective of whether they had cross-border establishments.

The agreement reached in 1988 was not binding because, like other agreements of this kind, no regulator was in a position to commit their national parliament to go along with what was agreed. Successive Basel Accords have been no more than a commitment by the parties involved to use their best efforts to procure the same outcome for each of their national jurisdictions. This, too, has been a source of continued tension, most recently when the US regulators, who had been amongst those bargaining most actively in the process, subsequently proved unable to secure ratification in the Congress of the agreement they had reached in Basel.

Since the first Basel Accord (Basel I), there has been a process of continuing periodic amendment to take account of the evolution of the markets, including most notably the greatly increased scale of trading activities, major developments in the field of securitization of bank assets and radical advances in the sophistication of banks' own risk management, not least to handle the creation and subsequent development of a range of increasingly complex derivative activities.

In 1996 the Committee issued the so-called Market Risk Amendment, designed to incorporate within the Accord a capital requirement related to the market risks arising from banks' open positions in foreign exchange, traded debt securities, equities, commodities and options. An important aspect of the amendment was that, as an alternative to a standardized measurement method, banks were permitted, subject to strict qualitative and quantitative standards, to use internal value-at-risk models as a basis for measuring their market risk capital requirements. Much of the preparatory work for the market risk package was undertaken jointly with securities supervisors with the intention that the methodology could also be used for non-bank financial institutions and particularly for the large securities houses.

In spite of this useful updating, there was an increasing sense in the late 1990s that the structure of the original arrangement was less and less fit for purpose. It was doubtful whether, because of its simplicity, it adequately reflected underlying risks, to the point where it delivered positively perverse results and was ill-suited to handle innovative techniques such as securitization. As a result, the more sophisticated banks, who used models of their own to make their business decisions, were frustrated that the regulators paid no attention to them. It became more and more obvious that economic capital – the reserves banks thought they needed to support their business – and regulatory capital were increasingly divergent.

Change was needed in three main areas. In the first place, the method for basic calculation of capital used in the first Accord was seen to be over-simple in relation to the variation in the risks of different kinds of instruments, with, for example, risks of manifestly varying quality receiving the same capital charge. However, deciding which new weight to give to which risk was challenging, and banks themselves had very different views. Secondly, it was judged important to be able to supervise the functioning of the banks' own risk management systems, especially if there were to be a move to using the numbers generated by the banks' own models in calculating regulatory capital. However, this involved the use of qualitative indicators and judgement, approaches familiar in some jurisdictions but regarded as constitutionally unreliable in others. Lastly, there was an increasing sense that more reliable results would be achieved through reinforcing the rule book approach of the regulators by exposing bank managements to market discipline and by making it possible for discipline to be exercised by the markets through enhanced disclosure of the underlying risk position of a bank. There were lively disputes about the most effective way to do this in ways which would be readily understood and would not produce destabilizing results.

In 1998 the Committee decided to proceed to a reform of the earlier arrangements. Some fundamental difficulties immediately emerged. In the first place, it became clear that an attempt to look at every possible kind of risk and to weight each separately quickly led to systems of extraordinary complexity. While it might be possible for the dozen or so most sophisticated banks in the world to build and operate complex models, clearly this was not possible for the vast range of banks to which regulators across the globe wished to apply the new regime.

Secondly, there was a question as to whether banks with more sophisticated risk management systems should as a consequence be permitted to run with lower levels of capital. Was it rational to offer incentives to banks to introduce more sophisticated systems by allowing them to hold lower capital when a bank with less sophisticated systems, but with an identical balance sheet, was required to hold a higher amount?

Third, there was a question as to whether the overall level of capital in the system, as well as its distribution, mattered. One school of thought held that, given that the existing level of capital in the system as a whole seemed about right, it would be risky to allow it to fall just because of a new system of assessment. Others argued that, if the new system was indeed more sensitive to economic risk, then regulators should be ready to accept the logic of the calculations that emerged, even if aggregate capital fell materially as a result.

Fourth, it was clear that the more risk sensitive capital requirements became, the more sensitive they were to the position in the economic cycle and hence the more likely it was that banks would react in a way which could itself accentuate the cycle. There was, therefore, a question as to how regulators should adjust for the resulting 'pro-cyclicality'.

Lastly, the number of stakeholders demanding to be satisfied had become more extensive. Legislators in both the US and the EU had woken up to the fact that arrangements they were expected to copy into national legislation were being negotiated by unelected officials. They started to intervene in the negotiations, encouraged by banks that sensed the wind was blowing in a direction they disliked. That was particularly true in the US and Germany. German politicians were especially nervous about the implications of a new Accord for bank lending to small firms, which they feared would appear more risky, and therefore requiring more capital backing than in the past.

In addition to the G10 countries directly involved in the negotiation, there was a wider world outside which had increasingly come to use the standards set by the Basel Committee as benchmarks to be introduced, albeit with adjustment to local circumstances, as widely as possible.

The Current International Regulatory System

The fact that the work done in Basel effectively set the standard for the world made it necessary for the Basel Committee to put in place new structures. The G10 Governors were, however, resistant to the idea of expanding the membership of the Committee itself.

The revision to the earlier Basel Accord involved an extensive process of consultation over six years. The very uncertain nature of the impact of the changes envisaged led to several rounds of impact assessments and consequent revisions to the draft proposals. The objective of the new arrangements is to strengthen the soundness and stability of the international banking system while maintaining sufficient consistency so that capital adequacy regulation will not be a significant source of competitive inequality among internationally active banks. A final set of proposals, known as Basel II, was finally agreed in 2004.

The approach is based on three complementary elements, or 'pillars' as they are known. These are:

Pillar I: Minimum capital requirements, based on the application of risk weights to the bank's assets. The Pillar I requirement includes capital to back credit, market and operational risks.

Pillar II: Supervisory review, which includes an assessment of the quality of a bank's systems and controls and risk management, and may result in an adjustment of the Pillar I capital requirement, either up or down.

Pillar III: Market discipline, including more stringent and detailed rules on disclosure and transparency.

The revision has kept to the basic requirement to hold total capital equivalent to at least 8 per cent of the risk-weighted assets, to the basic structure of the 1996 Market Risks Amendment and to the earlier definition of eligible capital.

The main innovation is the greater use of assessment of risks provided by banks' own internal systems as an input to capital calculation. A detailed set of minimum requirements designed to ensure the integrity of these internal risk assessments has been introduced. This leaves it to supervisors to judge how to determine a bank's readiness to use internal systems as part of the regulatory process.

A range of options for delivering the capital requirement for credit risk and operational risk allows banks and the supervisors to select the approach most appropriate for their operations and their financial market infrastructure. Banks may choose a so-called Standardized Approach (seen as appropriate for banks without sophisticated risk models of their own) or one of two approaches based on the use of internal ratings: the Foundation or Advanced Internal Ratings-Based Approaches (IRB). Unfortunately, as these three approaches are seen as indicators of sophistication, some countries whose banks are ill-suited to Advanced IRB are mandating its adoption.

An Accord Implementation Group (AIG) was established to promote consistency in the framework's application by encouraging supervisors to exchange information on implementation approaches. Home country supervisors have been given an important role in leading the enhanced co-operation between home and host country supervisors that will be required for effective implementation. The AIG has developed practical arrangements for co-operation and co-ordination intended to reduce the implementation burden on banks and conserve supervisory resources.

The framework establishes *minimum* capital requirements for internationally active banks. National authorities are free to adopt arrangements that set higher levels of minimum capital or use other supplementary capital measures such as a leverage ratio or a large exposure limit. This is to deal, for instance, with the potential uncertainties in the measure of risk exposures inherent in any capital rule or to constrain the extent to which an organization may fund itself with debt.

At least one hundred countries intend to implement Basel II, at varying dates.[2] In the European Union it is already incorporated into the Capital Requirements Directive. However, although agreement was reached in the committee after lengthy negotiation, including within the EU, lack of timely engagement by stakeholders within the US meant that it has not been possible to move smoothly to implementation there because a range of issues was reopened for debate. This has arisen in part because of the range of business models the Accord seeks to accommodate, although this is generally true for most jurisdictions. The issues which have surfaced, and which have been compounded by inter-regulator rivalries, have included the desire by some regulators to prevent capital falling below existing levels by putting in capital floors, or by continuing to use a leverage ratio, notwithstanding its lack of risk sensitivity. There has been an intensive debate on the extent to which US banks should be allowed to choose between the full range of approaches to be allowed in other jurisdictions or whether instead to use a specially tailored, more risk-sensitive version of Basel I, known as Basel IA.

At the same time international banks with operations in both the US and elsewhere have understandably been opposed to material divergence by the US, which will increase their own implementation costs, as also do timing differences. It was only as late as July 2007 that the four different US banking regulators finally reached agreement on the implementation of Basel II in the US. They agreed that the rules implementing the advanced approach should largely be consistent with international approaches and on a progressive phasing in of floors for reductions of capital subject to a review process. They also agreed to provide all non-core banks with the option to adopt a standardized approach under the Basel II Accord and to abandon the long-debated 'Basel IA' option.

As well as the specific project of setting capital requirements, the Committee worked to foster sound supervisory standards worldwide through the creation of 'Core Principles of Banking Supervision'. First adopted in 1997, these sought to provide a comprehensive blueprint for an effective supervisory system. Successive Latin American, Russian and Asian financial crises uncovered the fact that weaknesses in the overall structure of banking supervision were major contributing factors. These weaknesses included lack of independence, lack of authority and lack of resources on the part of supervisors. Partly they arose from inadequate tools of supervision. A Liaison Group was established to encourage countries to implement the Core Principles and a methodology was developed to assess the current state of a country's compliance.

Discussion has now returned to the issue of possible standards for liquidity risk management, an area where agreement on a single approach has long been difficult to reach and which remains a neglected part of the architecture. Adequate capital may not be sufficient to mitigate a liquidity crisis and may even give a false sense of comfort. There has historically been a mismatch between global management of liquidity by a financial group and the pattern of local regulation. Such local requirements may even increase the chance of firm specific or systemic cross-border problems and reduce the efficiency of consolidated liquidity risk management. There is a need for home and host regulators to co-ordinate and for arrangements for central banks to co-ordinate their approaches to eligibility of collateral for loans. At the same time such arrangements need to take account of what would or could happen in the event of insolvency.

The industry is itself working to help provide answers and the Institute of International Finance (IIF)[3] has been developing Principles for Liquidity Risk Management aimed at allowing the development of individual risk management practice and at avoiding quantitative, prescriptive requirements or additional capital requirements to offset heightened liquidity risk. The Joint Forum (see pp. 81–5) had identified large differences in national

47

requirements not obviously attributable to any particular business model and the Basel Committee, as well as the European Commission and the ECB, has been exploring ways in which to address this.

Deposit insurance

The risk that banks will fail and not be rescued has led governments to put in place schemes to reimburse retail depositors for losses. The world of deposit insurance is surprisingly divided. There are four separate, albeit overlapping issues on which different countries take markedly different positions.

The *first* question is whether to operate a deposit protection scheme for small depositors at all. The United States has had the Federal Deposit Insurance Corporation (FDIC), with a high profile, since the bank failures of the depression years. It was established in 1933 and proudly claims that since its foundation 'no depositor has lost a single cent of insured funds as a result of a failure'.[4] Most other developed countries also operate deposit insurance schemes of one sort or another. The European Union has a legislated minimum deposit insurance of around £30,000 per individual depositor. But countries such as Australia and Singapore long held out against the establishment of deposit insurance schemes, on the free market grounds that they create incentives against good risk management by banks, and promote moral hazard. There are also a number of developing countries where the banking system has been thought to be insufficiently mature to allow the establishment of a significant degree of deposit insurance for small savers.

But though the international trend is increasingly towards the establishment of deposit insurance schemes, there are three further issues on which countries are divided. The *first* of these is whether there should be any element of coinsurance built into the scheme, in other words whether the deposit scheme should guarantee 100 per cent of deposits up to a certain level, or require the depositor to take some element of risk, to promote market discipline, and to prevent large depositors parcelling up their savings into blocks which will then all effectively be insured. The US comes down on one side of this debate: the FDIC fully insures the first $100,000 of all depositors. The UK comes down on the other side, and while the first £2,000 of deposits are 100 per cent insured, the remainder up to the maximum of £33,000 is only insured as to 90 per cent. Following the Northern Rock problem in 2007 this arrangement is under review. The range of practice on this point in different countries remains highly diverse. In theory, an element of depositor discipline is attractive, but the political tolerance for depositor losses is low.

The second issue is whether deposits should be guaranteed by a fund, or simply by a regulator with the power to impose a levy on other banks in the event of a failure.[5] This is generally characterized as the difference between pre- and post-funding. Once again, the US and the UK have reached different conclusions. The FDIC has a fund which currently totals around $50 billion, which backs more than $3 trillion of deposits in US banks. The FDIC invests these funds largely in US government debt instruments. In the case of the UK there is no fund, and never has been. The existence of deposit insurance is of course, in principle, public knowledge, but is not advertised in the same high profile way as it is the US, where every radio commercial for a bank includes a reference to its FDIC insured status. The UK regulator has the power to impose a levy on other banks to pay for depositors' losses in the event of a failure. In recent years these failures have been typically so small as to impose no significant burden on the system as a whole, but even though there is the potential for a very large call on healthy banks, they remain in favour of a post funded scheme, on the grounds that pre-funding ties up capital in unproductive ways. The range of practice on this point in other countries is diverse and it is not possible to identify an emerging consensus.

Lastly, there is the question of whether, even if deposit insurance exists, there is a need for a separate entity to maintain it, and to supervise banks specifically for the purposes of protecting the deposit insurance fund. Countries which maintain pre-funding often also establish a regulator to protect that fund, while countries with post event funding normally argue that there is no need for separate supervision for deposit insurance purposes, and that the normal prudential supervision regime is adequate for that purpose. Once again, the US and the UK are on different tracks. The FDIC employs about 4,500 people, in Washington and around the country. It directly examines and supervises over 5,000 banks and saving banks, placing no formal reliance on the work of other supervisors such as the Federal Reserve Board, the Office of the Controller of the Currency, or the State Banking Supervisors. The existence of a separate supervisor for the deposit protection scheme may create inter-agency tensions. An entity solely concerned with protecting a deposit guarantee fund will be likely to seek early closure of a vulnerable bank, while a supervisor with a broader remit may be inclined to favour regulatory forbearance in the hope of restabilizing and recapitalization. These tensions have been observed in the US.

The contrast with the pre FSA Bank of England regime could hardly be more stark. Responsibility for UK deposit insurance rested with the Bank of England, but the Deposit Protection Scheme existed in virtual form, except for a board with a couple of commercial bankers on it. It was staffed by half an official and a small portion of a secretary. The Bank of England saw no need for separate supervision, relying on the work of its normal supervision and surveillance division. When the FSA was established, the government decided that the responsibility for administering deposit insurance should pass to the newly created Financial Services Compensation Scheme (FSCS), which also incorporated the previous policyholder protection arrangements in insurance and the investor compensation scheme in securities markets. (There are similar issues to resolve in relation to policyholder protection and investor compensation, but there are so far no international organizations in those areas.) But while there is now a separate entity (albeit in the character of a wholly owned but optionally independent subsidiary of the FSA) the FSCS relies exclusively on the FSA's supervision, and does not have any continuing relationship with banks. Only in the event of a failure would it deal directly with banks, through the imposition of a post-funding levy. This system is considerably cheaper to operate, but there are questions as to whether it provides the degree of consumer reassurance needed at times of stress.

There is, again, no international consensus on this point. In our view, in developed countries with a generally stable banking system there is little benefit, and considerable cost entailed, in a pre-funded regime with a separate regulator. The balance of argument is, however, different in some developing countries where confidence in domestic banks is low.

In 1999 the FSF established a working group on deposit insurance. The working group reported in September 2001 and proposed the creation of an International Association of Deposit Insurers (IADI).[6] That association was established in May 2002, and, while it is a separate legal entity, it is located at the Bank for International Settlements in Basel. The 'vision' of the association is 'to share deposit insurance experience with the world'. It seeks to do that by promoting guidance on the organization of deposit insurance systems and international co-operation.

Perhaps inevitably, since the establishment of an association of deposit insurers presupposes the existence of separate deposit insurers, the organization is dominated by countries which favour what might roughly be called the North American model. There are currently forty-four members, including the FDIC in the US, and the Canadian, French and Japanese deposit insurers. But the United Kingdom FSCS, and the German, Italians and Spaniards, for example, are not members. They have so far seen no particular value in joining an organization which presupposes a structural model which they do not favour. As its membership is biased towards developing countries, the organizational structure of the IADI reflects that dominance. So far, the Association has focused on the production of technical guidance to countries establishing deposit insurance schemes, and has prepared a useful survey of international practice – though one which illustrates the current diversity of views. Its attempts to address the cross-border dimension of financial safety nets have so far been modest in character.

A January 2006 paper entitled 'General Guidance to Promote Effective Interrelationships among Financial Safety Net Participants' did little more than exhort countries to consider the need for close co-operation and co-ordination across borders, while recognizing 'the possibility of conflicting mandates' and the difficulties of interface created by the existence of different legal and institutional arrangements in different countries.

The IADI has not addressed the practical questions of how the failure of a major retail bank operating on a large scale in a number of jurisdictions would be handled. Given its very partial global coverage, and the diversity of its membership, it is hardly in a position to do so. However, within the EU this issue is an increasing preoccupation, particularly where foreign banks constitute a major part of the banking system.

Payment and settlement systems

Payments and settlements systems are the essential plumbing of the world's financial markets. They are necessarily complex and sophisticated, as are the arrangements to oversee them.

As the BIS's own name implies, at the core of international collaboration in banking lie the basic technical arrangements for payments between banks and for the clearing and settlement of foreign exchange and securities transactions. If the arrangements are unsound or fail, even for the briefest time, cross-border financial markets could instantly face disruption which would transform the risk profile of participants and immediately have an adverse effect on the non-financial sector.

Since 1980, work has been undertaken to address issues which arise at the international level in relation to the soundness and efficiency of such systems. The Committee on Payment and Settlement Systems (CPSS) is a forum of central banks under BIS auspices which has evolved into a standard setter at the global level. In 2001, it issued 'Core principles for systemically important payment systems'.[7] They set out the ways in which such systems, which handle large-value, interbank payments, can protect themselves against risk and hence the wider financial markets from consequent systemic disruption.

The CPSS and IOSCO produced, also in 2001, 'Recommendations for Securities Settlement Systems' covering the design, operation and oversight of securities settlement systems and promoting the implementation of measures that improve the safety and efficiency of such systems, both at the national and cross-border level. In 2004 they published 'Recommendations for central counterparties' to cover the major types of risk faced by central counterparties, the entities which interpose themselves between the counterparties in a financial transaction, becoming the buyer to the seller and the seller to the buyer.

All these standards are intended to reduce the risk of malfunction in the most basic plumbing of the financial system, which other aspects of regulation tend to take for granted. While complex, they tend not to raise the type of political and distributional issues which arise in other areas of regulation, which makes international agreements somewhat easier to secure.

Money laundering: the Financial Action Task Force (FATF)

Financial institutions may be unwittingly (or wittingly) used as intermediaries for the transfer or deposit of funds derived from criminal activity. Criminals and their associates use the financial system to make payments and transfers of funds from one account to another; to hide the source and beneficial ownership of money; and to provide storage for bank notes or securities through a safe deposit facility. These activities which are associated with wider societal damage, such as drug trafficking, corruption, illegal arms trading, or financing of terrorism, are referred to as money laundering. Banks are the most likely conduits, through other types of financial firms have also been (mis-) used in this way.

Efforts have long been made by the authorities to prevent financial intermediaries being used for such purposes. Initially these efforts were in the hands of the law enforcement and judicial authorities at national level.

Financial firms often argue that they are merely passive agents in such laundering and cannot be expected to know the motives behind the myriad transactions undertaken by their customers. Banking supervisors themselves typically argue that their primary function is to pursue the overall soundness of banks and not to ensure that individual transactions by bank customers are legitimate.

However, the increasing international dimension of organized crime and of efforts to conceal the proceeds of corruption generated political pressure to address the problem at the international level. It also became plain that results could be achieved far more effectively if banks and other financial intermediaries actively sought to minimize the scope for the financial system to be used in this way. Banks themselves started to become concerned that public confidence could be undermined by adverse publicity as a result of inadvertent association with criminals. As a result, the Basel Committee in 1988 decided to promulgate some principles to help counter money laundering.

These principles were rather general and encouraged banks' managements to put in place effective procedures to ensure that all persons conducting business with them were properly identified; that transactions that did not appear legitimate were discouraged; and that co-operation with law enforcement agencies was achieved.

The concerns about money laundering continued to mount and the G7 Summit in 1989 established a Financial Action Task Force (FATF) comprising the G7 and eight other countries, plus the European Commission.[8] The FATF was given the responsibility of examining money laundering techniques and trends, reviewing the action that had already been taken at a national or international level, and setting out the measures that still needed to be taken to combat money laundering. In 1989 the FATF issued a report containing a set of Forty Recommendations, which were intended to provide a comprehensive plan of the action needed to fight against money laundering. Since then the membership has expanded to a current 33 members. The FATF has updated the Forty Recommendations to reflect the changes that have occurred in money laundering and terrorist financing techniques and has conducted several rounds of mutual evaluations amongst the member jurisdictions.

The FATF standards encompass the following aspects; customer identification; ongoing monitoring of accounts and transactions; record keeping and reporting of suspicious transactions; internal controls and audit; integrity standards; and co-operation between supervisors and other competent authorities.

Parallel to the work of the FATF, the Joint Forum (see pp. 81–5) co-ordinates the work of the banking, insurance and securities supervisors in this field.[9] This cross-sectoral co-ordination is necessary because, to the extent that institutions in each sector are offering the same services, anti-money laundering/terrorist financing measures need to be reasonably consistent, otherwise there would be a tendency ('criminal arbitrage') for criminal funds to flow to institutions in sectors operating under less stringent standards. At the same time, variations in the pattern of relationships between institutions and customers require adaptations to the rules for each sector.

These measures have been widely incorporated into national legislation and regulation with increasingly specific and demanding requirements as public concern has mounted about criminal and terrorist activity. Especially since 11 September 2001, there has been increasing disquiet as to whether the results in terms of criminal action impeded or terrorist attacks thwarted warrant the cost and bureaucracy involved for banks and their customers. In particular, there is considerable doubt as to whether the law enforcement authorities have the capacity to analyse and act on the vast volumes of reports received on suspicious transactions. Retail customers are also frustrated by the burdensome requirements associated with account-opening and new investments. Nonetheless, while the terrorist threat remains intense, and it is apparent that acts of terror can be financed with relatively small sums of money, these obligations – like intrusive airport security – seem likely to remain in place. How effective they are remains open to doubt: few prosecutions for the underlying offences have arisen from suspicious activity reports submitted by banks.

Securities markets

International Organization of Securities Commissions (IOSCO)

The parallel organization to the Basel Committee in securities markets is the International Organization of Securities Commissions (IOSCO).[10] To date, IOSCO has had a somewhat lower profile than the Basel Committee. That is, in part, because the cross-border issues faced by securities regulators have been less central than those in banking and because the conduct of business issues in which it deals are less all-pervasive than the overall risk management and capital allocation rates dictated by Basel. It may also be because securities regulators initially saw themselves as under an obligation to preserve those features of their national market which were thought to promote some special competitive advantage and only discovered later that they too needed to rely on each other to deal with enforcement across borders, and to devise approaches to meet challenges which are inherent in all markets. (This is set out in some detail by Sloan and Fitzpatrick in their discussion of the structure of international markets regulation in Financial Markets and Exchange Law.)[11] That is now changing, as securities markets are dominated by a small number of global intermediaries, and as the exchanges themselves become part of broader international groups. The takeover of Euronext, which already included the domestic markets in France, the Netherlands, Belgium, Portugal and the UK futures market, by the New York Stock Exchange in 2007 underlines the importance of cross-border understandings on the nature of securities and derivatives market regulation. NASDAQ subsequently bid for OMX, the Scandinavian Baltic Exchange, while the London Stock Exchange took over the Borsa Italiana. Further consolidation of the stock exchange sector seems likely.

IOSCO itself grew out of an association of the stock exchange commissions of the Americas set up in 1974. At a conference in Quito in 1983 it was agreed that other countries could join the organization, and that it would become a global body. In the following year the United Kingdom, France, Indonesia and South Korea were the first group of new countries to join. Since then, effectively all securities regulators have become members, with also an associate category of membership for offshore centres, for second regulators in the same country as a full member (e.g. the CFTC) and for other affiliates including exchanges themselves.

IOSCO is organized on more democratic and representative lines than the Basel Committee. All members are in the President's Committee, which must ultimately ratify agreements and codes, while the Executive Committee, which oversees the secretariat and the organization's finances, is elected, and the membership changes from time to time. However, the IOSCO group which most closely parallels Basel, the Technical Committee, is a self-perpetuating group, with a membership which shows traces of the organization's origins in the Americas. The US have two members, the SEC and the CFTC, as does Canada, with both the Ontario and Quebec Commissions occupying separate seats. There is, however, somewhat broader representation in the IOSCO Committee than in Basel. Hong Kong and Mexico are among the members, and the Chair of the IOSCO's Emerging Markets Committee attends as of right. Below these top-level committees is a complex network of sub groups (see Chart 4).

The Technical Committee has developed most of IOSCO's regulatory policies over the years, with the detailed work undertaken by Standing Committees which report to it. There are now five such committees, covering Disclosure and Accounting, Secondary Market Regulation, Market Intermediaries, Enforcement and the Exchange of Information, and Investment Management.

The vastly greater diversity of membership, coupled with the fact that chairs of securities regulators typically have shorter tenure than governors or heads of supervision in central banks, has made it more difficult for IOSCO to achieve consensus, even on matters much less complex than the Basel Accords, and hence to agree standards which raise the quality of securities regulation internationally. There have on occasions been tensions within IOSCO between emerging market representatives and others. That was true, for example, when the organization sought to analyse what had happened in the Asian financial crisis, and in particular to look at the role hedge funds played at that time. Nonetheless, in recent years its achievements have been significant.

Chart 4   *IOSCO Structure*

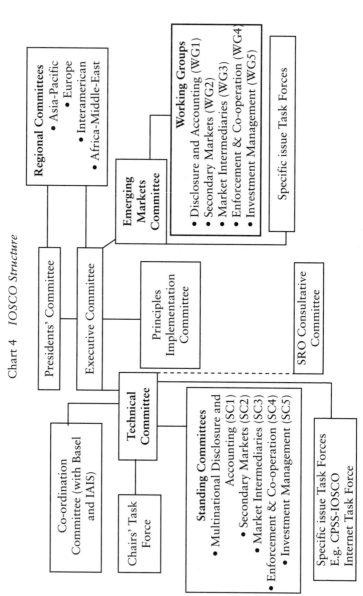

Source: Adapted with permission from Sloan and Fitzpatrick in Chapter 13, The Structure of International Market Regulation, in Financial Markets and Exchanges Law, Oxford University Press, March 2007

The organization describes its members' objectives in the following terms:

- to co-operate to promote high standards of regulation in order to maintain just, efficient and sound markets;
- to exchange information on their respective experiences in order to promote the development of domestic markets;
- to unite their efforts to establish standards in an effective surveillance of international securities transactions;
- to provide mutual assistance to promote the integrity of the markets by a rigorous application of the standards and by effective enforcement against offences.

A general statement along these lines begs many questions. What is meant by 'just, efficient and sound markets'? What is 'effective surveillance', and how do we define market integrity?

In an attempt to answer these questions somewhat more precisely IOSCO agreed, in 1998, a comprehensive set of objectives and principles of securities regulation, known as the IOSCO Principles, which are now recognized as the benchmarks of international regulation of securities markets. Those principles have been used by the IMF since 1999 in undertaking their financial sector assessment programmes, although IOSCO itself did not establish an assessment methodology to evaluate implementation in individual countries until 2003, when the principles themselves were overhauled.

The Current International Regulatory System

The second pillar of the IOSCO universe is the multi-lateral memorandum of understanding, adopted in 2002. While in many circumstances securities markets are competing against each other for mobile business so may not always wish their regulators to standardize regulation internationally, increasing concern about cross-border securities fraud or other misbehaviour provides a strong incentive for regulators to collaborate. Many pairs of countries have in the past agreed bilateral MOUs on the exchange of information, but there was previously no standardized framework for such MOUs, resulting in a confused and confusing patchwork of understandings, which were difficult to operate effectively and rapidly in the case of an investigation of doubtful or connected transactions. In many cases the signature of the MOU is followed by nothing more than a glass of champagne, with the document itself quickly consigned to a locked filing cabinet, but there have been occasions in recent years when the lack of a good legal underpinning for information exchange has hindered effective enforcement. In some countries, the law requires regulators to impose obligations of confidentiality on other enforcement agencies to which they pass information. In many cases the different domestic freedom of information, individual data protection and disclosure regimes do not easily map against each other. This is a considerable weakness at a time when traded markets are increasingly global.

The IOSCO multilateral MOU was a bold attempt to create a standardized framework which would facilitate information flow. Progress towards expanding the signatories of this MOU has, however, been slow. Only in 2005 did IOSCO members commit themselves to achieving broad coverage, and then not until 2010. As at the end of 2006, only 34 of the 108 full members of IOSCO had signed up to the MOU. The leadership of IOSCO was showing some frustration with the slow progress. The chair of the Executive Committee, Jane Diplock of New Zealand, said in October 2006 'frankly, it is imperative for regulators to have greater cross-border reach if we are to remain effective in the globalized securities markets'.[12] This was a further example of the difficulty of reaching agreement in an organization based on consensus, and relying only on the best endeavours of individual members to implement IOSCO standards and codes domestically.

So, while IOSCO has undertaken a good deal of useful work of a comparative nature on, for example, the ways in which hedge funds are regulated (or not) in individual jurisdictions, or credit ratings agencies, or the rules in place to promote independence of securities analysts, and auditors, much of the resulting work is largely descriptive in character. There have been few occasions on which IOSCO has itself achieved an enhancement of regulatory standards internationally. The SEC's lukewarm commitment to the organization has not always helped. SEC chairmen have typically not personally attended the Technical Committee, although other country's regulators are almost always represented by their chairs. That undoubtedly has the effect of devaluing the status of the Committee. And the SEC's commitment has tended to depend on the enthusiasm of the individual commissioner assigned the international brief.

The Current International Regulatory System

It is fair to say, too, that in recent years European securities regulators have placed a greater emphasis on, and have contributed more wholeheartedly to, the development of European-wide regulatory agreements in the Committee of European Securities Regulators (CESR) (see below). However, now that the New York Stock Exchange owns four domestic European cash equity and derivative markets as well as the London International Financial Futures Exchange (LIFFE) and with other cross-border mergers under discussion, IOSCO may gain a new lease of life. Cross-border agreements on information exchange and on regulatory standards will be of greater practical significance in the future, and IOSCO could provide the forum in which such agreements can be reached if the main players allow it. Concern that the regulation of US markets may itself be damaging their own competitiveness has also led to greater American openness to dialogue on international issues.

Stock exchanges

Stock exchanges may also become affiliate members of IOSCO, and many do so. They also typically join their own association, the World Federation of Exchanges, formerly the FIBV (Federation Internationale des Bourses de Valeurs). In 2001 the name was changed to reflect the expansion of its membership to include derivatives exchanges.

The WFE cannot properly be regarded as a regulatory group. It is not represented at the FSF. Its exchange members vary in terms of their regulatory responsibilities. Most undertake some form of front-line surveillance of trading patterns, but some pass evidence of unusual trading to the securities regulator for action, while others have their own investigative and disciplinary powers. Many still have listing responsibilities, although these have increasingly passed to independent regulators.

So the WFE is a trade association, rather than a regulator, though part of its mission statement records that its work

> enhances the co-operative relationship with supervisory authorities, in order to advocate the benefits of exchange front-line self-regulation within the total regulatory framework and the process of international mutual recognition.[13]

The WFE has fifty-seven members, now including NASDAQ, who joined only in 2006. Members are required to meet certain minimum standards to qualify as an organized market, but those standards are generally below those which would be required for legal recognition in most developed countries. The WFE has, however, played and still plays a role in raising operational and regulatory standards in exchanges in developing countries.

Credit rating agencies

Credit rating agencies perform a crucial function in international capital markets and potentially provide

the first line of defence for investors. Almost all significant borrowers, whether corporate or sovereign, have
a rating issued by one of the two major agencies,
Moody's, and Standard and Poor's. The same agencies also rate individual debt instruments, including
many derivatives. These ratings, in turn, are used by
regulators to assess the quality of portfolios held by
banks or securities firms, and the associated capital
reserves needed. Under Basel II, the importance of these
ratings will grow, especially in the more sophisticated
versions.

The agencies themselves have not been subject to the
kind of regulatory attention paid to securities firms or
banks. Only in the United States have they enjoyed any
form of official recognition. In 1975 the SEC began
to designate agencies as nationally recognized statistical rating organizations (NRSROs). There were five
NRSROs: AM Best (which principally covers the insurance market), Dominion Bond (a Canadian bond rating
agency) and Fitch IBCA, together with the two majors.
But this status as a nationally recognized agency did
not carry any implication that the SEC approved
ratings methodologies, or carried out any regular oversight of the way the agencies operate. And in other
countries there was no comparable registration, though
in some cases regulators have used the SEC recognition
status as a proxy for deeming rating agencies to be
appropriate for the purposes of ratings used in capital
requirements.

The failure of Enron in October 2001 threw a harsh
spotlight onto the agencies and their work. Until very

shortly before its collapse Enron was highly rated. Congressional hearings in the US were held, and the rating agencies pressed to explain why they did not downgrade the company earlier. The agencies themselves defended their position, arguing that the information provided to them by Enron was deficient and in some cases fraudulent. But this did not fully offset the political pressure. Attention began to focus on the extent to which the market is a comfortable duopoly, on high barriers to entry and the lack of effective competition, on the integrity of a process in which companies pay for their ratings, and on other market practices such as downgrades for derivatives if the underlying security is not rated, which some argue to be anti-competitive. (The sub-prime crisis added further concerns about the extent to which the agencies were involved in advising firms on how to structure credits to achieve higher ratings and about their lateness in downgrading those credits.)

Against that background, politicians in the US argued that the agencies should be directly regulated by the SEC, and their internal processes controlled in some way. Others, including the SEC itself, were reluctant to go down that path, concerned about the implications of official approval for ratings, and the potential liability on regulators and the government in the event of failure. There was tension between those who argued for more official oversight, and those who believed the official sector should retreat from such oversight as there was, and that it was the existence of the NRSRO status in the US, which implied some official regulation of the agencies without delivering it effectively, that was the problem. This was an uncomfortable dilemma for international regulators, especially at a time when banking supervisors were proposing, under Basel II, to place greater reliance on the agencies' work than before.

The period from 2002–6 therefore saw a range of attempts to resolve this dilemma, both in the United States and internationally. A clause in the Sarbanes–Oxley Act required the SEC to review the role and functions of credit rating agencies and the operation of capital markets. But the SEC's initial report did not point to any clear conclusions about future regulation. Reviews in Europe of the regulation of ratings agencies produced a similar 'unproven' verdict. Majority opinion among the regulators was that the agencies should themselves be responsible for policing conflicts of interest, and ensuring the integrity of their analysis. IOSCO published a code of conduct on rating agencies which set out some useful principles, but did not propose any new activities by regulators themselves.

This did not satisfy the US Congress and after considerable debate the Credit Rating Agency Reform Act of 2006 was signed into law by President Bush before the mid-term elections in October 2006. The Act abolished NRSRO status, but created a new status of Statistical Rating Organizations and gave the SEC authority to impose requirements on the agencies for being granted such status. However, it did not give the SEC regulatory authority over the rating methodologies used by the agencies themselves. As it was passed,

Senator Richard Shelby, the outgoing Chair of the Senate Banking Committee, said the Act would deal with the conflicts of interest and lack of competition which had been seen in the rating agency sector in the past.

It is not yet clear how far this legislation will, in practice, alter the environment within which the agencies operate. While Standard and Poor's, in particular, opposed the legislation, they and Moody's have not seemed excessively concerned by its passage. The SEC, however, has not yet explained how they will implement the Act, so there could be tensions ahead. And the further unsignalled failures in the subprime sector will put pressure on the Commission and on regulators elsewhere to adopt a more intrusive approach in the future. Meanwhile, in the EU debate continues about the criteria for acceptance of rating agencies' judgements as part of Basel II implementation and this has renewed concern about the potential conflict between the role of rating agencies in providing advice on the structuring of an instrument which they may then go on to rate. There is also concern in Europe about the role rating agencies play in the credit derivative market: at French insistence the FSF established a review of market practices in 2007. In August 2007 the Commission launched a further review. We certainly cannot be sure that the regulation of rating agencies has now reached a stable resting place. The fall-out from the sub-prime crisis may well have altered the political balance, in favour of more intrusive regulation in the future.

Insurance regulation

IAIS

While the Basel Committee was established in 1974 and IOSCO in 1983, it was not until 1994 that the International Association of Insurance Supervisors (IAIS) came into being.[14]

Insurance markets remained nation-based for longer than securities markets, and the requirement for ring-fenced funds to back life insurance policies, often supported by special domestic tax arrangements, in particular, reduced the possibility of cross-border contagion arising from the failure of a fund in an individual country. Also, most insurance supervisors were historically parts of Ministries of Finance, or – as in the UK case – the Department of Trade and Industry (as it then was). Many were not constructed as distinct, independent authorities with the capacity to conduct their own 'foreign policy', so to speak. In the US, insurance regulation remains a state competence. The National Association of Insurance Commissioners is a voluntary federation of fifty separate Commissions or Superintendencies, and therefore ill-equipped to exercise global leadership (see pp. 166–7).

By 1994 a critical mass of countries were ready to acknowledge that interdependencies were growing, and that there was a case for an Association with the capacity to develop principles and guidance, and to promote best practice. Its aims are succinctly expressed:

- to contribute to the improvement of insurance supervision for the protection of policy holders
- to promote well-regarded insurance markets, and
- to contribute to global financial stability.

This last aim was added after the creation of the Financial Stability Forum in 1999, which for the first time brought the IAIS into discussions which identified the potential impact on financial stability of problems in global insurance and reinsurance markets. Reinsurance is insurance for insurers. While all countries directly regulate insurance companies which sell policies to clients, whether private or corporate, in the case of reinsurance some countries regulate directly, and some indirectly through regulation of retrocession contracts in place between insurers and reinsurers. Still others do not regulate reinsurers at all. (See 'Reinsurance and Financial Markets: Group of Thirty Report,[15] published in 2006, for an extensive discussion of the regulation of reinsurance. The Group of Thirty is a private non-profit international body established in 1978 and composed of very senior representatives of the public and private sector and academics who form a consultative group on international economic and monetary affairs.)

The arrival of the FSF also had a broader impact on the IAIS, stimulating more rapid and energetic work on standards and codes, which began to be used by the IMF in its FSAPs (see pp. 119–26) from 2000 onwards. There is now a set of IAIS core principles, a 'roadmap' for achieving them, a 'framework' and a set of 'conventions' for implementation. These mixed metaphors together describe a substantial body of useful work. There is no doubt that the status of the IAIS has recently been enhanced, and its membership coverage has broadened. At the end of 2006 the Association represented 180 jurisdictions in 130 countries (the difference reflecting the fifty separate jurisdictions in the US: a continued anomaly), with coverage of 97 per cent of worldwide insurance premium income. Nonetheless, habits of co-operation between insurance regulators are not well-entrenched. Many domestic regulators were (or in a few cases still are) parts of government ministries who saw their international role as marginal.

The governance structure of IAIS is quite similar to that of IOSCO. Ultimate authority rests with the General Meeting of all members, with an elected Executive Committee overseeing the work of the Technical, Implementation and Budget Committees. The Technical Committee establishes global insurance regulatory and supervisory standards, working through a range of sub-committees and task forces.

IAIS members have worked over an extended period to develop non-binding core principles of insurance supervision, much along the lines of those drawn up by Basel and IOSCO. These cover the essential principles that need to be in place for a supervisory system to be effective, including licensing criteria, the key elements of on-going supervision and prudential requirements. Supporting this is a suite of thirteen supervisory standards on a range of issues such as licensing, on-site inspections, fit and proper requirements, evaluation of reinsurance cover of primary insurers and investment risks. The principles and standards are supported by a further dozen guidance papers as well as educational material designed to assist supervisors. These cover subjects as broad as public disclosure, the use of actuaries as part of the supervisory process, investment risk management and risk transfer.

IAIS followed the other supervisors and in 2007 drew up a Multilateral Memorandum of Understanding on Cooperation and Information Exchange. Notwithstanding the historical separation of national insurance markets they are now influenced by the increasing integration of financial markets and the growing number of internationally active insurance companies. Like other such MOUs, the MOU does not supersede any national law or create any legally binding obligations, but it does rely on strict confidentiality regimes being in place to protect information exchanged.

However, only slow progress has been made towards achieving common standards for the assessment of insurance solvency, weaknesses in which had become increasingly evident in the face of unreliability and volatility in the assessment of liabilities and greater understanding of the extent to which asset values could also fluctuate.

In 2006, IAIS agreed on a roadmap for creating a common structure for assessing insurance solvency. The first step is to improve the transparency of the existing solvency arrangements and of the financial condition of individual insurers and next to work towards convergence of solvency regimes. The common solvency structure, set out in detail in February 2007, will encompass three blocks of material: financial, governance and market conduct.

By contrast to banking, much of the concrete work on insurance standards, and particularly on solvency, is being driven forward within Europe. When agreement is reached there, this is likely to lead the way over time towards convergence at the global level. The EU project goes by the name 'Solvency II' and is a fundamental and wide-ranging overhaul of the existing ('Solvency 1') suite of directives affecting both life and non-life insurers and reinsurers. This updating is driven by the need to update requirements which have their roots thirty years ago. The existing regime has been demonstrated to be insufficiently sensitive to risk, to the point where some jurisdictions, such as the UK, have had to introduce supplementary regimes to ensure more realistic assessment and management of capital. The new framework is intended to make solvency requirements much more risk responsive and to take better account of major advances in risk management, including capital modelling techniques.

Insurance supervisors have decided that they can appropriate the framework developed for banking for their own purposes and the intention is that, as in Basel, there should be a three pillar structure of minimum capital requirements, supervisory review and reporting and disclosure. It will cover convergence of standards for the valuation of technical provisions for liabilities and more risk-sensitive capital requirements, including a better recognition of risk mitigation techniques. It will also cover the use of a firm's internal models for the calculation of capital requirements, and the ability of supervisors to require additional capital under Pillar II following a supervisory review process. Substantial further work still needs to be done and implementation is unlikely before 2010.

Reinsurance

There has been a long debate about whether reinsurance should be regulated and, if so, how. It is a core element of the insurance system, potentially contributing to the soundness of primary insurers through allowing them to reduce the level of risk they retain on their own balance sheet and so the impact of adverse shocks on their financial position. Through facilitating the diversification of primary insurers' risk exposures, it allows them to separate origination from portfolio composition.

Notwithstanding the global nature of the business, which is concentrated in just eight jurisdictions, some of them offshore, regulation has traditionally been undertaken at a national level, if at all, with little consistency of approach across jurisdictions, and consequently with heavy reliance on rating agencies as de facto regulators. This led to concerns about the extent to which the reinsurance industry is a potential source of systemic risk for the financial system as a whole, about the role of securization and the links between insurance and the capital markets, about the adequacy of the industry's transparency and indeed about the adequacy of the regulatory arrangements.

Although the Group of Thirty Study Group concluded that some of these concerns were probably exaggerated, nevertheless it concluded that regulation, as well as transparency, could be improved. Within the EU a Reinsurance Directive was agreed in 2005 which brings greater consistency to the assessment of reinsurance solvency. The G30 recommended that, given the global nature of the business, regulators needed to develop a more harmonized regulatory approach across countries. In particular, they recommended that supervisors worldwide adopt an approach that reviews the condition and activities of reinsurance groups on a consolidated basis, utilizing risk-based capital standards. Although the likely absence of systemic significance and the wholesale nature of the business meant that the regime for regulation could not derive directly from the rationale for banking, one similarity between reinsurance and banking is the importance in both industries of group structures in managing risk.

One of the building blocks to improving insurance regulation lies in the adoption within the framework of International Financial Reporting Standards (see pp. 91–4) of consistent accounting standards for insurance contracts, still some years off. Current accountancy practices are diverse and often differ from accounting approaches in other sectors. Harmonized regulatory valuation standards are central to the introduction of solvency standards and accounting, economic and regulatory measures of capital need to converge.

The Current International Regulatory System

Actuarial standards

Sound accounting is in turn dependent on sound actuarial input where there have been major shortcomings in recent years, including in the core area of longevity, where many insurers (and pension funds) have underestimated the impact on their solvency of increases in life expectancy. Currently there are no international actuarial technical standards to stand alongside those in the accounting and auditing fields, nor indeed any formal structures in place to generate them, although the International Actuarial Association (IAA) promotes co-operation between national actuarial associations and sets some standards in the educational field. Since technical actuarial standards are the province of the profession in most jurisdictions, no potential independent international standard setter exists. However, public interest oversight of the standard setting process has been introduced in countries like the UK and the steps being taken there and elsewhere to bring core principles to bear to the setting of actuarial standards will need to develop into moves to generate international standards, particularly as cross-border insurance groups need to develop a consistent group-wide approach to risk assessment and measurement.

Such standards will need to apply greater objectivity, reliability, relevance and consistency than has hitherto been the case in addressing central actuarial concepts such as value, risk and forecasting, including mortality. If consensus emerges on the need for international actuarial standards, which we think it should, an oversight structure will need to be created which adequately provides legitimacy, both in terms of independence and accountability.

International Organization of Pension Supervisors

Although the soundness of pension provision is of vital importance to individuals, its regulation is less well developed as a separate discipline than that in the banking, securities and insurance fields. This is because much pension provision is directly undertaken by government or else undertaken through the medium of insurance or investment vehicles, often supported by special tax benefits. Separately funded private occupational arrangements nevertheless exist in many countries and are often subject to regulation, sometimes by one of the other financial regulators, typically the insurance or integrated prudential, as in the Netherlands, but also stand alone, as with the Pensions Regulator in the UK (formerly the Occupational Pensions Regulatory Authority (OPRA)), which is not part of the FSA.[17]

Because of the key role played by national tax arrangements the question of co-operation between regulators to handle cross-border operations is much less of an issue than with other regulators, but the need has still been felt for an international organization to provide a worldwide forum for policy dialogue. The International Organization of Pension Supervisors (IOPS), formed in 2004 out of an earlier informal network, has around sixty members and observers from fifty countries.[18] It acts as a standard-setting body on pension supervisory matters, promotes international co-operation between pension supervisors and other groups in improving the quality and effectiveness of supervision and undertakes statistical work and research.

It is run, rather like the IOSCO, by an Executive and a Technical Committee and has a secretariat serviced by the OECD. Its work covers the study of a risk-based approach to pension supervision, licensing of pension funds, supervisory education, guidelines on off-site supervision and good governance of pension funds. More formal arrangements, underpinned by legislation, operate within the EU, and are described in Chapter 4.

Cross-sectoral problems: the Joint Forum

It became gradually apparent during the 1990s that there were a growing number of issues which were common to the banking, securities and insurance sectors, in particular the regulation of financial conglomerates with activities in all three. To recognize that gap the Basel Committee, IOSCO and IAIS established, in 1996, the Joint Forum which is made up of an equal number of bank, insurance and securities supervisors representing both their respective parent committees and their national constituencies. It has met 3 times a year since its inauguration and representatives come from 13 countries, 9 from Europe (the EU Commission is also present as an observer) plus the US, Canada, Australia and

Japan.[19] The Forum's secretariat is provided by one part time member of the Basel Committee secretariat.

To address financial conglomerates issues, the Forum was asked to provide guidance on information sharing, on capital adequacy, risk concentration etc. It has also been specifically charged with looking at the structures of financial conglomerates that may impair effective supervision, to assess the appropriateness of group-wide methods of supervision and develop guidance and principles in that area.

However, concrete progress on financial groups' supervision at the global level proved elusive, mainly due to political resistance in the US in particular, and to the long-standing resistance of the large US investment banks to group supervision of any kind. Nonetheless, the Forum's work initiated a momentum for change and the EU took the lead in implementing the Forum's recommendations by setting out legal requirements for the supervision of cross-sectoral groups in the Financial Groups Directive. This included a provision which effectively excluded from EU markets groups from non-EU jurisdictions which lacked adequate group supervision. The Directive generated the impetus necessary to overcome the resistance in the US to reform and co-operative arrangements were agreed between the US regulators to put in place oversight of group-wide systems and controls and capital requirements.

While the original motivation for establishing the Joint Forum was the growth of financial conglomerates, its work has not been restricted to their regulation. The Forum has been tasked with looking at risk areas that are

Box 1   Credit Derivatives

Increased transfer of credit risk between financial firms has been watched closely by public authorities in the last decade. In 2003 the Financial Stability Forum asked the Joint Forum to examine the extent and nature of credit risk transfer, with a focus on credit derivatives.

Credit derivatives allow credit risk, traditionally the domain of banks, to be shifted around the financial system more easily and cheaply than before. As this risk crosses the boundaries of banking, insurance and securities it offers a useful example of the benefits of cross sectoral co-operation and action.

As an over-the-counter market the only way to get a grip on activity is through engagement with the full range of relevant regulated counterparties. The Joint Forum was able to work with firms across the sectors it represents to provide a somewhat clearer picture of the credit derivatives market and where credit risk was ultimately held. It was also able to spot supervisory issues relevant to all its members and where collaboration was required. Prudential issues, risk management and the potential for market abuse were all raised as were more mundane, but important, operational issues such as the importance of matching and confirming trades in a timely fashion. The result was a set of recommendations that were equally important for supervisors of banks, insurance companies and securities firms and which no one sector could have determined in isolation.

> Nonetheless, the market crisis of 2007 once again raised questions about the ability of supervisors to track the movement of credit risks around the system.

common to all sectors, such as anti money laundering, outsourcing, operational risk and risk aggregation – the approach used by firms to manage and aggregate risks across different businesses. The Forum has also been asked to look at the cross-sectoral implications of extreme exogenous shocks, including the way in which regulators might come together in those circumstances to co-operate and co-ordinate their responses. And financial innovation has forced supervisors to collaborate where risks traditionally concentrated in one sector, such as credit risk, are transferred around the financial system.

This is, potentially, an extensive remit. But the Forum depends on the authority and policies of its parent committees. It cannot take initiatives without a specific mandate from its creators and even existing work streams do not always end with detailed and meaningful recommendations – its credit risk transfer report being a notable exception. Instead the Forum is frequently restricted to investigative studies with open outcomes. National sensitivities are at work. But the sectoral focus of the Forum's creators also plays a significant part. The result is that mandates and outcomes can be watered down to the lowest common denominator, potentially missing the opportunity to tackle unnecessary (and expensive) differences in sectoral approaches to common issues, to enhance best practice across sectors and to effectively address remaining gaps in the system. In Chapter 7 we discuss ways in which the Joint Forum could usefully be strengthened.

Financial reporting

All financial markets, and hence all financial regulators, rely on the existence of meaningful and reliable financial information. The supply chain for corporate reporting consists of a number of elements involving both the preparers and auditors of financial statements. At the start come the accounting standards, which need to be decided upon and implemented by the company preparing the accounts. Then come the auditing standards, which need to be decided on and implemented by auditors who need to be licensed, supervised and, if necessary, disciplined. This whole process needs to be supervised through proper corporate governance arrangements for which there are codes including the provision of adequate oversight of the preparation and auditing of financial statements.

Most countries have agreed arrangements of varying degrees of formality for some or all of the links in this supply chain. Historically these arrangements have been voluntary on the part of the companies or delivered through self-regulation by the accounting and auditing professions. However, with mounting concern over the reliability of both accounting and auditing, these arrangements have increasingly been placed under independent public oversight, though without any systematic pattern across countries. In only one country, the UK, is there an integrated authority, the Financial Reporting Council, covering all the elements, which in the UK case extends to the oversight of the actuarial profession and setting of actuarial standards. In other jurisdictions standard setting and oversight is spread across a range of bodies, public and private.

Auditing

As financial markets have become more international so has concern about the extent to which foreign regimes for financial reporting can be relied on or provide the basis for accurate comparison of financial statements of companies from different jurisdictions.

The audit market globally is very concentrated, with the vast bulk of audits of public interest entities, including financial institutions, concentrated in the hands of four very large and two somewhat smaller firms. In fact, these are not firms or groups in the sense that banks or insurance companies comprise branches or subsidiaries legally linked to a holding company. They are instead virtual organizations, taking the form of networks which articulate the relationship between the various legally separate national partnerships which comprise them through the granting of a franchise in return for an expectation that they will conform to standards of behaviour and collaborate in the provision of services to international clients.

Historically, the audit industry has been self-regulating, sometimes under loose surveillance from trade or justice ministries. However, after a raft of scandals, notably but not exclusively in the US, there has been a rapidly spreading movement to establish independent regulators of the audit profession. Post-Enron the US established the Public Company Accounting Oversight Board (PCAOB).[20] Other countries, like Canada and the UK, quickly followed suit with similar bodies and the EU has decided that from 2008 all member states will have independent audit oversight bodies.

The creation of this added layer of protection for investors immediately raised questions about whether domestic investors should have the same level of protection in relation to both domestic and foreign companies listed on the domestic stock exchange.

The Sarbanes–Oxley legislation in the US requires the PCAOB to carry out oversight of auditors in foreign countries who audit the accounts of companies listed on US stock exchanges. This approach was then adopted by the EU in its 8th Company Law Directive, partly in an attempt to push the US to relax the Sarbanes–Oxley requirements, and Japan has now followed suit. The overlapping jurisdictions thereby created have raised the nightmare prospect of competing troops of audit regulators from many jurisdictions descending on audit firms in up to a hundred countries to undertake extraterritorial registration and inspection, very often in languages other than their own. Discussions have only recently begun to see whether a way can be found to make it possible for regulators to place mutual reliance on each other. To get to this position much still needs to be done, even assuming national legislators will accept the general proposition.

It would be easier to move to mutual recognition if there were agreed international standards for the regimes for oversight of auditors, but they do not exist. International Standards on Auditing have been created by the International Federation of Accountants (IFAC),[21] but they have not been endorsed by the audit regulators, still less put into effect in many major countries.

Standard setting for audit remains an anomaly in that there is no regulatory body at the international level. This is partly because the setting of audit standards is still in most jurisdictions dominated by the accounting profession. Because of the concern the various groups of financial regulators had about leaving the creation of the international standards to the profession, they banded together with the World Bank and the EU to form a Monitoring Group which in turn created in 2005 a Public Interest Oversight Board (PIOB)[22] to oversee reforms in IFAC's own processes to ensure that its policies, processes and procedures all served the public interest. This the PIOB now does – through the oversight of the processes of IFAC's International Auditing and Assurance Standards Board (IAASB) and its companion ethics and auditor education standard-setters. It does not, however, determine the content of the standards, which remain for final decision by the IAASB.

The Current International Regulatory System

The International Forum of Independent Audit Regulators

For a number of years before the creation of independent audit regulators, IOSCO had been active in making recommendations for improvements in the audit field, but the creation of independent audit oversight bodies in a number of jurisdictions led to the creation in 2006 of the International Forum of Independent Audit Regulators (IFIAR).[23] Because of the critical role of sound audit in all financial regulation, all the three major financial regulatory organizations (Basel, IOSCO and IAIS) are observers at IFIAR.

Thus far IFIAR has confined itself to exchanging information and experience, and to fostering co-operation, with no ambition to set core principles or standards for audit oversight, unlike its more mature counterparts in banking, securities and insurance. In any case, more fundamental issues need to be tackled first, including the basic need for cross-border exchange of information, already the staple of co-operation between other financial regulators. This is fundamental because the audit files which need to be inspected will for most companies relate to business in numerous foreign jurisdictions. Similarly, the audit firms being overseen will often form part of one of the global audit firm networks. These networks exercise a powerful influence over audit quality across the globe and their brand reputation is crucial. At the same time the global firm's international networks remain outside national oversight. IFIAR will need to decide how national regulators can collectively address this gap in the oversight system, whether through some sort of college or a form of consolidated supervision.

This gap is potentially important because the high degree of concentration in the market makes it vulnerable to the loss of one or more of the networks because of contagion arising from a major financial or legal hit to part of the network and a confidence run leading to loss of clients of the kind which destroyed Arthur Andersen after Enron. Loss of a further firm could lead to a hiatus in the supply of the high quality auditing services on which financial markets and their regulators rely.

While auditing standards provide conduct of business rules, like those elsewhere in financial regulation, there is no comparable prudential regime to assess audit firms' risk management systems or to judge whether they have adequate financial reserves or insurance. Given the reliance placed on audit for the regulation of financial firms and of markets, we believe there is a case for prudential regulation of audit firms at the national level and for a form of collective consolidated supervision to be exercised over the global networks.

Other ways of mitigating the risks caused by the current structure of the global audit market involve opening up the ownership structure to new entrants and to additional capital, and perhaps to limiting civil liability so that it is no more than proportionate to any failings directly attributable to the conduct of the audit firm. The work already begun in these areas on both sides of the Atlantic should be pressed forward and appropriate reforms introduced.

The Current International Regulatory System

The need, discussed above, to establish a basis on which audit regulators can place reliance on each other when registering auditors of foreign listed companies is also likely to drive IFIAR sooner or later in the direction of the creation of core principles for audit oversight.

International accounting standards

The search for a set of agreed accounting standards which all internationally active companies can use, providing the basis for comparability across jurisdictions, is the regulatory equivalent of the Quest for the Holy Grail. Such standards would provide a common standard for investors and regulators and eliminate the need for expensive and confusing reconciliation.

In the late 1960s accounting standard setters in the US, the UK and Canada set up a working group to examine the possibility of agreeing a set of common standards. That work led to the creation of the International Accounting Standards Committee in June 1973.

For the next quarter of a century the IASC worked on a wide range of technical communications, known as International Accounting Standards (IAS), covering most of the major issues arising on corporate accounting. But in spite of this huge volume of technical work a number of important issues remained difficult to resolve, and standard setters in individual countries, notably in Europe and the US, were reluctant to accept IAS as a legitimate replacement for, or alternative to their own standards. The SEC, in particular, was suspicious of the IASC, and concerned that it was too vulnerable to political influence, especially from the European Commission.

A period of introspection and review at the end of the 1990s led to a new structure for the IASC, which was designed to insulate the international standard setters from political interference, and to enhance confidence in their work. So in March 2001 the IASC Foundation was established. The Foundation was to act as the parent of a new and better-resourced International Accounting Standards Board, based in London.[24] The Foundation, with twenty two members, is there to appoint the Board, to protect its independence, and to secure funding for its work.

To agree the membership of the new Foundation a small committee of regulators and accountants was established. This group agreed to invite Paul Volcker to chair the Foundation, with Sir David Tweedie, the head of the UK's Accounting Standards Board, as first Chair of the IASB itself.

In April 2000 IOSCO, at its annual conference in Sydney, had agreed in principle to recommend International Accounting Standards for cross-border listings, subject to satisfactory reform of the structure and process. And in September 2003 a European Commission Regulation required the adoption by EU companies of International Financial Reporting Standards (IFRS), as the new standards were to be known, from 2005 onwards. A large number of other countries have similarly resolved to mandate the adoption of IFRS.

In spite of this strong political support, and energetic leadership from David Tweedie, progress has not been easy. The funding arrangements, with support coming largely from the major accounting firms and major corporations, proved controversial. The Board has found it difficult to agree standards on fair value accounting and on accounting for financial instruments, facing political opposition, including from the then French President Jacques Chirac. The European Commission refused to take up its seats on the Foundation. Partly as a result of this political controversy, full adoption of IFRS, especially in the US, has proved elusive. An agreement between the IASB and the US Financial Accounting Standards Board (FASB) in October 2005 re-affirmed that 'a common set of high quality global standards remains the long-term strategic priority of both the FASB and the IASB'. But the words 'long-term' and 'strategic' illustrated that achievement of this priority was still a long way off.

In an unfortunate echo of the Middle East Peace process the two sides agreed a 'roadmap' to guide them towards the removal of the current need for foreign companies in the US to produce a reconciliation statement showing how their accounts would appear under US GAAP, even if they are prepared in line with IFRS. The SEC noted that the removal of the reconciliation requirement would depend on further progress on several fronts.

Wholesale market players started to argue that the difference in standards in practice was well understood by market participants and this started to raise the possibility that both US Generally Accepted Accounting Principles (GAAP) and IFRS could be accepted in the US. Meanwhile, the EU had instituted a rule requiring non-EU issuers on EU markets to use IFRS-equivalent accounting standards by 2007. The impracticability of this has caused the deadline to be put back by two years and it may have to be put back again.

However, in 2007 US concerns about the competition of their financial markets, reinforced by the growing reluctance of foreign firms to list in New York, began to prompt a concrete interest in IFRS. SEC Chair Christopher Cox forecast the acceptability of international accounting standards by 2009, announced a proposed rule change that would mean that foreign firms would no longer need to reconcile to the US GAAP, and published a concept release which raises the possibility that even US firms might be allowed to use IFRS in the future. If carried through, these changes would amount to a major breakthrough. It remains to be seen what consequences they would have in other major jurisdictions, but they are a step closer to a single set of global accounting standards. It remains to be seen if IFRS will effectively drive US GAAP out of the market. This may depend on the extent to which IFRS itself can remain a unified set of standards once it has gone through the process of adoption by each national jurisdiction. In any case IFRS ought to continue to evolve so as to generate the best possible set of standards, without having convergence with any one national GAAP as a goal in its own right.

Corporate governance

Financial regulation relies implicitly on sound corporate governance, whether for the purpose of putting in place and operating sound risk management systems or to generate reliable financial statements. At the same time, financial regulators rarely have responsibility at national level for corporate governance, which touches on far wider interests. As a result, although financial regulators have collective views on what constitutes sound corporate governance for their industry segment, international work on principles of corporate governance has primarily been undertaken elsewhere, largely by the World Bank, the OECD or, in the EU, by the European Commission.

The political sensitivity of the issues at stake and the substantial differences in social and business structures has generated a reluctance to reach agreement on implementing an agreed international standard in detail. The international standards or principles which exist serve as benchmarks rather than rules. Even between the US and the UK there remain sharp divisions. In the US a combined Chairman/CEO is the corporate norm: in the UK such an arrangement is strongly discouraged under the code of practice currently in force. In much of continental Europe two-tier boards are the norm.

The OECD Principles of Corporate Governance,[25] originally endorsed by OECD ministers in 1999, provide guidance for legislative and regulatory initiatives. The FSF has designated these 'Principles' as one of the twelve key standards for sound financial systems and they underpin the corporate governance component of Work Bank/IMF Reports on the Observance of Standards and Codes (ROSC).

The OECD Principles focus on governance problems that result from the separation of ownership and control.

They cover the following areas: (i) ensuring the basis for an effective corporate governance framework; (ii) the rights of shareholders and key ownership functions; (iii) the equitable treatment of shareholders; (iv) the role of stakeholders; (v) disclosure and transparency; and (vi) the responsibilities of the Board. But while these principles are sound, they will not in themselves create greater standardization of international practice, which remains highly divergent. Does this matter? Perhaps not, but it does mean that financial regulators in 'host' countries have to rely on risk management in parents which are not governed on lines of which they would normally approve.

Consistent corporate governance standards have not been agreed at the international level because of significant differences both in the legal approach to imposing corporate governance requirements and in views on their content.

In some jurisdictions corporate governance requirements are set out in legislation and enforced through the courts or by securities or other regulators. In others they are set out, at least in part, through codes which are, strictly speaking, voluntary. Companies are then expected either to comply with the relevant code or give a reasoned explanation as to why they have not complied with them. Such 'comply or explain' requirements may be included in exchange listing requirements. This approach gives companies flexibility to determine their governance arrangements in the light of the precise circumstances in which they find themselves at any point in time while giving shareholders the opportunity to express their views on the decisions a company takes.

The Current International Regulatory System

As noted above, there are significant differences in view between, or even within, jurisdictions as to some of the key structural elements of governance. Most continental European countries prefer a two-tier board structure, under which there is a management board, essentially consisting of executives of the company, and above that a supervisory board, predominantly composed of non-executives. While this puts in place a division of responsibility and accountability, it may also be unwieldy and inefficient. Furthermore, the supervisory board is typically chaired by the previous CEO, creating opportunities for second-guessing the firm's executive management.

A unitary board avoids those risks. But there are other risks, notably of an excessive concentration of power, especially where the Chairman is also the Chief Executive. Combining the two roles may make for clarity in management and accountability. To an over-dominant individual it may also remove a potential source of restraint. For that reason UK practice has moved decisively in favour of a split between the Chairman and the CEO. The former is clearly acting in the interests of shareholders, and those interests may sometimes diverge from the interests of management, notably in the case of a takeover bid. There are signs that opinion on this point is beginning to shift in the US also, after a number of scandals involving over-powerful CEOs who confused the company's finances with their own. But most major US corporations are still led by a single individual holding the combined role of Chair and CEO.

There are also differences of view over the size of the board and the role the non-executive directors are expected to play, including whether a senior non-executive should be designated to provide leadership if it should be needed.

A further major difference in approach derives from shareholding structures. Where shareholdings are widely spread, as is often the case in the US or UK, a key objective of governance arrangements is to seek to curb the excessive power which management might wield by virtue of the challenge shareholders face in mobilizing themselves to affect the strategic direction of company executive remuneration or other matters of vital interest to shareholders.

When shareholdings are concentrated it is easier for dominant shareholder groups to influence the management, but they may do this in ways which are not in the interests of minority shareholders. In such cases a key corporate governance concern will be how best to balance the interests of different shareholder groups.

Against this background of lack of agreement on common approaches, a single set of governance standards at the global level seems a remote prospect. Nevertheless, there is an increasing sense that, while comparable accounting and auditing approaches are helpful in promoting the soundness of cross-border capital markets, without sound corporate governance, investors' interests may still be prejudiced. We thus expect debate about the best models for corporate governance internationally to intensify. There is, for instance, likely to be pressure for greater convergence from global investors, with New York or London investors expecting to see similar governance arrangements in companies they invest in elsewhere.

The rapid growth of private equity funds poses a different kind of challenge. Private companies are not subject to corporate governance requirements set by exchanges or regulators. That is worrying to trade unions and employees generally, who fear that management in private equity-owned companies will take an excessively narrow view of their responsibilities. There is no obvious solution to that problem, if it is one. (We discuss the regulation of private equity in Chapter 7.)

Islamic finance

Islamic finance is one of the fastest growing elements of the international financial system. Estimates of the total size of the sector are hard to gauge, but a figure of around $300–500 billion of outstandings is likely in 2007. What is clear is that the growth rate is rapid, perhaps as much as 50 per cent a year in the last five years. Not all of the growth is occurring in Muslim countries. Islamic mortgages are common in the UK, and the British government has announced its interest in issuing a shariah-compliant bond, a sukuk.

In most countries, so far, Islamic finance sits alongside conventional financial products and services, although one or two countries have determined that they will move the whole of the financial sector onto an Islamic basis. Essentially, Islamic finance must be consistent with Islamic law principles. In particular, Islamic law prohibits usury, the payment of interest (commonly called Riba in Islamic discourse) and trading in financial risk. There are also further prohibitions related to investments in businesses, such as those selling alcohol or pork, which are contrary to Islamic values. In order for it to operate in compliance with Islamic principles, a financial institution must establish a Shariah Board of experts in Islamic law who are responsible for ensuring that the products and business practices of the firm are fully compliant with the law as they see it.

These characteristics of Islamic finance pose novel challenges for regulators. In the past, the international groupings have not addressed them. Indeed, as the authors of a recent book 'Islamic Finance: the regulatory challenge' point out, 'Basel II was not written with its application to Islamic banking in mind'.[26]

There are six areas in which it is necessary to adapt the international regulatory regime to the particular demands of Islamic finance:

Capital

Pillar I, the calculation of minimum capital requirements under Basel II, does not explicitly cater for Islamic products. In principle, since Islamic products do compete directly with conventional equivalents, it ought to be possible to establish a degree of risk equivalence between them, but there are, so far, exceptions to this rule. Under European directives, for example, mortgages have been treated differently when offered by an Islamic institution, with a higher capital allocation required. (In an Islamic mortgage transaction the bank acquires the property and writes a finance lease with the ultimate purchaser, so it is directly exposed to the risk of loss on the property.) The Islamic Financial Services Board (IFSB), established in Malaysia in 2002, has produced a capital adequacy standard for all Islamic products, which is rooted in Basel II and which seeks to interpret the principles of Basel II and adapt them to an Islamic environment.[27]

Deposits

Since Islamic banks are unable to pay interest, customer deposits are normally constructed as a kind of profit sharing contract, known as Mudarabah. In principle, the customer enters into a risk sharing arrangement with the bank, related to an underlying parcel of assets. This creates issues in relation to deposit protection schemes. As 'deposits' in Islamic banks are not capital certain, they cannot be treated in the same way as conventional deposits. They are effectively shares, in that they are remunerated by profit-related capital growth. There are also important questions of transparency and disclosure, since small shareholders of this kind are vulnerable to changes in the bank's circumstances in a way conventional depositors are not. The IFSB is developing a standard on transparency and market discipline to address those issues. In relation to deposit protection schemes, the UK has adapted its scheme to treat deposits in Islamic banks as analogous to share holdings in credit unions.

Other jurisdictions have not yet adapted their arrangements to include them.

Legal risks

The interaction between regulation and commercial law on the one hand, and Shariah law, on the other, can create particular legal risks. Customers may seek to evade obligations by claiming non-compliance with Shariah law. The British courts have recently rejected such a claim, but the fact that it was brought shows that the risk is there.

Corporate governance

While, in principle, it is clear that the Shariah Board's responsibilities are limited to assessing compliance with Islamic law, there is clearly the potential for overlapping jurisdictions and control systems within a financial institution. Regulators are likely to pay particular attention to the interface between the two control systems. They will wish to satisfy themselves that risk, asset and liability management are the responsibility of the main Board.

Reputational risks

Given that an Islamic bank's business model depends on ensuring Shariah compliance at all times, there is evidently a need for sharp focus on these decisions. A bank which was viewed as non-compliant could rapidly lose its customer base.

Operational risks

As with all financial institutions, operational risk is crucial. It is particularly significant in Islamic financial institutions, since the relevant IT systems and software are at a relatively early stage of development.

All of these issues pose challenges for regulators, and indeed for the international regulatory system. (See a useful chapter by Toby Fiennes in Archer and Rifaat[28] for a lengthier discussion.) The IFSB is addressing these issues in a systematic way. In December 2005 it issued two prudential standards for Islamic banks, one on capital adequacy and one on risk management, together with the draft of a third on corporate governance. The challenge facing the Board is to develop a framework which is applicable to all jurisdictions. That is not straightforward, given the different ways in which Islamic finance has been implemented in different countries and – in some cases – the relatively poorly developed systems of financial regulation in those jurisdictions. Also, the Board's remit was extended only at the end of 2005 to cover securities and insurance markets.

As Islamic markets develop it will be crucial for the international regulatory bodies to work more closely with the IFSB, in an attempt to ensure that the latter's standards are as compatible as they can be with best practice in conventional finance. At present, the links between the IFSB and the other regulatory bodies are underdeveloped and informal. In future, the IFSB will need to be brought more closely into the workings of the Basel Committee and elsewhere. It is hard to imagine, given the scale of Islamic finance today, that another capital accord could be developed without taking account of the particular needs of Islamic banks, as the Basel II Accord was. (For an insightful discussion of the issues see 'Islamic Finance and Financial Policy and Stability', by Andrew Sheng.)[29]

Offshore centres

The regulatory problems of offshore financial centres have preoccupied a number of international groups over the last fifteen years.

In fact there is no universally accepted definition of an offshore financial centre. Critics tend to regard them as places in which firms and individuals avoid paying tax, and certainly many have become significant on the back of very light tax regimes. The IMF offers a more neutral definition of an offshore centre, identifying three key characteristics:

1. large numbers of financial institutions which engage primarily in business with non-residents
2. financial systems with external assets and liabilities out of proportion to the financial intermediation needed to finance their domestic economies

3. some or all of the following: low or zero taxation; moderate or light financial regulation; banking secrecy and anonymity.[30]

In practice, these characteristics can be combined in both positive and negative ways. As the Financial Stability Forum report on offshore centres, published in 2000, observed 'the term offshore carries with it in some quarters a perception of dubious or nefarious activities. There are, however, highly reputable OFCs which actively aspire to comply with international best practices, and there are some legitimate uses of OFCs. OFCs are not homogeneous and there is a wide variety of practices found in them'.[31]

Whatever the precise definition, offshore centres have enjoyed a business boom in the last two decades. The OECD estimate that offshore holdings of financial assets are now between $5 and $7 trillion, five times as large as they were two decades ago.[32] The Cayman Islands, for example, is the world's fifth largest banking centre, and it and a number of other offshore centres are very large hosts of private banks and asset management companies. Many hedge funds have also established themselves, largely for tax reasons, in offshore centres.

Financial market development has stimulated economic growth in offshore centres, and some of them are now among the most prosperous countries in the world. But there have been disadvantages elsewhere. The OECD has focused on the tax losses to other countries of OFC activity. One NGO, the Tax Justice Network, estimates lost tax revenues at more than $250 billion a year.[33] These taxation issues are beyond the scope of this book.

But OFCs have attracted attention also from the financial regulators. The Financial Action Task Force (see also pp. 55–9) drew up a 'blacklist' of territories which it saw as non-co-operative in the global effort to reduce money laundering and restrict terrorist financing.[34] In 2000, 15 jurisdictions appeared on the list, almost of all them offshore centres, led by the Bahamas and the Cayman Islands. This blacklist focused the minds of regulators in those centres, as did the events of 11 September 2001. As a result, by 2006 all these jurisdictions had been removed from the list, following changes to legislation and improvements in supervisory practices.

But money laundering is not the only concern expressed by financial regulators in onshore jurisdictions. It was argued that offshore centres posed risks for financial stability, in that flows of funds to and through them were difficult to track. Efforts to prosecute insider dealing offences and other forms of market abuse were frequently handicapped by the lack of transparency in OFCs. These concerns prompted the Financial Stability Forum to establish a working group to look at the quality of financial regulation in those centres.

The working group, whose report in 2000 proved highly controversial in OFCs, identified three categories of centre. The first were centres in which regulatory standards were broadly compatible with those operated in onshore jurisdictions. The second was a group of centres which were close to compliant with international standards and codes, but where there were material deficiencies in some areas. The third group was a list of essentially non-co-operative centres, where compliance with international standards was limited. The report recommended that the IMF should, in view of the potential threat to the global financial system, carry out a systematic assessment programme designed to identify the shortfalls in regulatory standards, centre by centre. These assessments should be published.

The IMF accepted this recommendation, and included offshore centres in the financial stability assessment programme (see pp. 119–26). By the end of 2006, almost all the OFCs had been reviewed in some way by the IMF, and opportunities for improvement and reform identified. As a result, in early 2005, the Financial Stability Forum formally withdrew its list of the good, the bad and the ugly, which had become a bone of contention with many OFCs since its publication five years before.[35] However, the Forum noted that, while reforms had been initiated by many OFCs, there remained problems of compliance with international standards in several jurisdictions, particularly in the area of cross-border co-operation and information exchange. It established a review group on offshore financial centres, including the IMF, to monitor progress and advise on any necessary follow up actions.

There is little doubt that these efforts have improved the quality of regulation in a number of centres. They have not had a material impact on the tax incentive to locate offshore, but that is a separate issue. However, offshore supervisors remain somewhat semi-detached members of international regulatory groupings. They are members of IOSCO and IAIS, albeit not represented on the key committees. There is a group of offshore bank supervisors, which includes only those who are compliant with Basel standards, but they have no formal locus within the Basel Committee structure. And, while the international exposure generated by anti-money laundering efforts, and by the Financial Stability Forum, has somewhat altered the balance of advantage for offshore centres in favour of an approach built on a reasonably high standard of regulation accompanied by low taxation, there is no guarantee that the balance of advantage will not shift back again in the future.

Integrated regulators

At the initiative of the Australian prudential regulator, APRA, an informal group of the heads of integrated cross-sectoral regulators met for the first time in Sydney in the spring of 1999.

There is, as we explain elsewhere (see pp. 189–91), no simple definition of what is meant by an integrated regulator and, indeed, the Australian system is better characterized as a 'twin peaks' system than as full integration. So determining the appropriate membership of this group was not straightforward. The early meetings were attended by the Scandinavian countries, including Iceland, together with Singapore, the UK, Japan, Korea, Australia and Canada. More recently others like Austria, Germany, Ireland and Hungary have been added.

The Group, which meets annually, reaches no formal conclusions and has no official status. Its discussions have tended to focus on the practicalities of running a cross-sectoral regulator rather than on the rules themselves. (It is curious that the other international groups rarely, if ever, visit this important territory.) A sign of its significance is that the chairs typically do attend meetings, and the numbers are small enough to allow for a genuine exchange of views. It has conducted surveys on staffing levels, reward structures, skills and training. Over time, as the numbers grow, it may well become a more important network. Certainly it plays a role in ensuring that those new-style regulators learn from each other's experiences, and mistakes. Many innovations in regulatory techniques, especially the development of risk-based regulation, are now to be found in the integrated organizations.

3

The International Financial Institutions and their Role in Financial Regulation

The last decade has seen a major expansion of the role of the International Financial Institutions (IFIs), especially the International Monetary Fund and the World Bank, in the regulatory area as the impact of the condition of countries' financial infrastructure on the functioning of the real economy has become clearer.

Financial Stability Forum

The sudden and dramatic Asian financial crisis of 1997–8 came as a blow to the IFIs, who had not seen it coming. The post mortems of that crisis still continue today and controversy continues to rage over the extent to which the structural policies of the International Monetary Fund contributed to the problems, or indeed worsened them after the crises struck. Much bad blood has been spilled in sometimes ill-tempered arguments advanced by Professor Joseph Stiglitz for the prosecution, and better-mannered responses from the former number two at the IMF Stanley Fischer (now Governor of the Central Bank of Israel) for the defence.

It was clear, albeit after the event, that one important reason why the crisis turned out to be as severe as it was related to the position of the financial sectors in the affected countries and to the inadequacy of their regulation. (That may be the only point on which both sides agree.) Domestic banks in Thailand and Indonesia, in particular, were borrowing dollars at low international interest rates, and on-lending in domestic currencies. This was good business, while it lasted, as domestic interest rates were significantly higher. But the banks concerned ran large exposures to companies which themselves had large unhedged currency exposures. In some cases there was, in addition, a maturity mismatch, with short term borrowing backing longer-term loans. So when the currency pegs in place failed to hold (whether or not as a result of aggressive speculative activity by hedge funds is neither here nor there) the banks concerned were, effectively, bankrupt. That would have been so whether or not the borrowers themselves could pay in local currency. (A number of corrupt and doubtful loans did not help.)

Neither the IMF nor the World Bank had previously focused much attention on the weaknesses in financial regulation. Their emphasis had been largely on monetary and fiscal policy. Some of the countries concerned looked in a reasonably stable fiscal position in those areas, but with a fixed exchange rate clearly were extremely vulnerable to financial shocks.

111

Analysis on these lines caused many to ask whether some new institutional arrangements were necessary to strengthen the surveillance of global financial markets. It was argued that, while the regulatory groupings in place (Basel, IOSCO etc.) could articulate principles and codes of practice, they had no authority to enforce those codes. And neither the IMF nor the World Bank had hitherto seen financial regulation as being at the core of their activities. Article IV assessments of individual member countries by the IMF staff had typically paid little attention to the quality of financial regulation or the institutions in an individual country established to oversee it.

Some argued that to fill this gap a new institution was needed. There were proposals for a World Financial Authority with the ability to enforce good practice and, indeed, perhaps to intervene to restabilize markets where financing flows looked to have created severe vulnerabilities. Within the world's major finance ministries, plans for reforming the international financial institutions were developed. Gordon Brown was a leading proponent of reform. As chairman of the International Monetary Fund ministerial steering committee, now called the International Monetary and Financial Committee (IMFC), he was well-placed to take the lead.

But agreement on a new institutional framework proved elusive. Instead, in October 1998 the Finance Ministers and Central Bank Governors of the G7 commissioned Hans Tietmeyer, the former President of the Bundesbank, 'to recommend new structures for enhancing co-operation among the various national and international supervisory bodies and international financial institutions so as to promote stability in the international financial system'.

Hans Tietmeyer consulted widely and, in February of the following year, presented a report to the G7 recommending the creation of a Financial Stability Forum.[1] The Forum would include the national authorities responsible for financial stability in the G7, namely finance ministries, central banks and supervisory agencies, as well as representatives from other major financial centres such as Hong Kong, Singapore, the Netherlands, Australia, and now Switzerland. It would also include the sectoral groupings of regulators engaged in developing standards and codes, the international financial institutions themselves, and representatives of the committees of central bank experts concerned with market infrastructure and financing – the Committee for Payments and Settlement Systems, for example. The then General Manager of the Bank for International Settlements, Andrew Crockett, was appointed the first Chairman of the Forum in a personal capacity. A small secretariat, led by Svein Andresen, was set up within the BIS in Basel. (The second Chairman was Roger Ferguson of the US Federal Reserve. By 2007 the FSF was chaired by Mario Draghi, Governor of the Bank of Italy.)

In some countries, deciding on the identity of the regulatory member of the Forum was straightforward, especially where, as in the UK, there is a single authority. In others, such as the US, some tension resulted from the requirement to field only three representatives. So, for example, neither the Office of the Controller of the Currency or the CFTC, who are present in Basel and

IOSCO respectively, have a place at the table. In addition to the national authorities there are 6 seats for the international financial institutions, 2 each for the IMF and the World Bank and one for the BIS and the OECD. The European Central Bank, also turned up uninvited at the first meeting and has never been shown the door. By contrast, the European Commission declined to become involved in the process and has never become a member.

The objectives of the Forum are described as being 'to promote international financial stability, improve the functioning of the financial markets and reduce the tendency for financial shocks to propagate from country to country, thus destabilizing the world economy'.

The objective is to be pursued in three ways:

- assessing vulnerabilities affecting the international financial system;
- identifying and overseeing action needed to address these vulnerabilities; and
- improving co-ordination and information exchange among the various authorities responsible for financial stability.

The Forum meets on a plenary basis twice a year, and since 2001 has also held regional meetings with non-member financial authorities in Latin America, in the Asia Pacific region and in Central and Eastern Europe and Africa.

This mandate seems, at one level, quite straightforward. But it begs the question as to how far the Forum needs to commission its own work, and how far it should simply act as a clearing house, and perhaps as a stimulus to the work of others. At the outset, the first Chairman took the view that there were issues which existing groups were not handling with due expedition, perhaps because they were not ideally structured to do so. He therefore proposed the establishment of working groups of the FSF, which would report directly to the Forum itself, and through it to G7 finance ministers and governors. The first three groups established were focused on the implications for financial stability of the activities of highly leveraged institutions (primarily hedge funds), the risk posed to financial systems by offshore financial centres, and the potential instabilities created by capital flows, particularly those between developed and developing countries.

These new working groups produced reports over the following two years, which reflected the combined perspectives of different types of institution which typically did not work together. But in doing so they generated some controversy among existing institutions and existing groupings. How could their recommendations be implemented, if they were not supported by a parent with the authority to do so? What legitimacy did these groups have? How did their work relate to work underway in the more long standing committees and institutions?

These new questions have proved difficult to answer. And, while at least 2 of the 3 reports did produce recommendations and actions which strengthened the financial system (one of the authors of this book was Chairman of the Highly Leveraged Institutions Group, and is therefore perhaps predisposed to make this point), since this early wave of new initiatives the Forum has typically avoided establishing working groups of its own. No subject-specific working groups have produced reports since 2001. The Forum's publications now consist primarily of a series of status reports on 'ongoing and recent work relevant to sound financial systems'. These useful documents, published twice a year, are covered by a note which highlights and summarizes those initiatives started the previous six months. They are now an essential point of reference for any regulatory authority.

The Forum also produces what is described as a 'vulnerabilities' assessment as background for each meeting, which is designed to highlight potential risks in the global financial system.

The evolution of the FSF illustrates the difficulty of co-ordination and institutional change in a very complex environment. The FSF has not met some of the ambitious aims foreseen for it when it was established in early 1999. It did not prove possible for it to carve out a distinctive position, integrating the various perspectives of the diverse membership, as was originally hoped. It has no executive authority or power to mandate others. Commitment to the Forum by different members has been uneven. Some countries, notably the United States, have consistently argued that the Forum should not take initiatives of its own and it has tended to focus more on commissioning work from other relevant groups, such as on reinsurance or credit derivatives.

On the other hand, the compilations and compendia produced by the FSF are undoubtedly useful. Even large regulatory authorities in individual countries sometimes find it difficult to keep track of all the initiatives under-way. The vulnerabilities exercise itself is useful in focusing minds, although it has not always distinguished clearly between vulnerabilities which regulators can conceivably correct (for example regulatory overload) and those, such as global trade imbalances, which are beyond their reach. And the Forum, in establishing habits of co-operation between finance ministries, central banks and regulators may have enhanced their capacities to respond collectively in the event of a serious crisis. Whether it would be allowed to play a role itself in crisis management, however, will depend on the G7 finance ministers and central bank governors at the time. It is not clear that they would wish to see the FSF acting as the co-ordinator of international initiatives, even though it is the only body which groups together all the actors needed in the event of a serious bout of instability.

What is undoubtedly true, however, is that the existence of the Financial Stability Forum has given added impetus to the work of the individual sector–based regulatory groupings. Both IOSCO and IAIS, in particular, have become much more exposed to finance ministries, central banks and the international financial institutions and the same will probably become true of IFIAR. They are now aware of high-level political interest in their work. There has, as a result, been a noticeable quickening of the pace of their activities, on the one hand, and a notable upgrade of their focus on enforcement, on the other. In both cases, the obligations of membership have become more serious and burdensome in recent years.

That is undoubtedly a net gain. The Forum has also helped to educate Ministries of Finance on financial stability issues.

More generally, and perhaps with the most practical impact, the FSF provided the impetus for the push described below to use the IMF and World Bank to pressure countries to implement standards for financial regulation which had been created by the regulatory groupings, and to which in theory they were already committed.

The International Monetary Fund and the World Bank

The establishment of the FSF was not the only significant change implemented at the end of the last century.

Before the financial crises of the late 1990s, the roles played by the IMF and the World Bank in financial regulation were modest. The Fund paid some attention to the health of the financial sector in its Article IV assessments of member countries, and the Bank focused some of its technical assistance effort on financial sector institutions. But improving regulatory standards, and enforcing the standards and codes in existence, were not seen as central priorities.

The Asian financial crisis, and the realization that weakly regulated financial systems could contribute crucially to financial and economic meltdown led the G7 finance ministers (and others) to call on the Fund and the Bank to increase their focus on strengthening the financial systems of member countries, identifying vulnerabilities

118

at an earlier stage and highlighting development needs, especially in emerging markets.

So in 1999 the two institutions jointly established the Financial Sector Assessment Programme or FSAP (not to be confused with the EU FSAP, the Financial Services Action Plan), and the Standards and Codes Initiative (or ROSC – Report on the Observance of Standards and Codes). As an IMF evaluation paper published in January 2006 noted, the FSAP was introduced to fill an identified gap in the international financial architecture in support of crisis prevention, based on the judgement that existing surveillance approaches at the IMF under Article IV were not sufficient for effective financial sector surveillance.[2]

The programme of work undertaken under the FSAP by the Fund and the Bank has been very extensive. By the end of 2005 111 country assessments had been undertaken. In the case of developed OECD countries the IMF has generally carried out the work alone, albeit involving regulation experts from regulators in other countries. In the case of developing countries the work was undertaken jointly with the World Bank.

Most major countries have now been assessed, though with the important exceptions of China and the US. As the IMF laconically observe 'The gaps are primarily because the authorities of the countries concerned have been reluctant to participate in the exercise.' China has now agreed to participate: the US continues to delay. In view of the GAO's own critical assessment of the US system (see below), there is clearly a risk that an FSAP would identify gaps and weaknesses in the US arrangements, which would prove awkward for the Administration. It is nonetheless disappointing that the US has refused to participate for so long.

The IMF's own evaluation reports the average cost of each country report at $668,000, excluding overheads. These costs were reduced following a review in 2003 which recommended more selectivity, by focusing on the most relevant issues in each country.

In the case of large countries the costs were considerably higher. Thirty-eight people descended on the UK's financial authorities (primarily the Treasury, the Bank of England and the FSA) in 2001, from all corners of the world, for several weeks. And these costs do not take account of the associated effort of the staff in the countries being assessed. Japan estimates that 10 per cent of the staff of the J-FSA were engaged in the work at some time.

The focus of the assessments has been primarily on the extent to which countries are implementing the Standards and Codes put in place by international regulatory bodies, ranging from the IMF's own Code on Fiscal Transparency to the OECD's Principles of Corporate Governance. The twelve main blocks are described in Box 2. They also include assessments of the country's capability to address crisis and stress testing of the financial system as a whole.

In most, though not all, countries the resulting reports have been published, at least in summary form, allowing market participants and others to reach their own views on the quality of regulation in place. In theory countries should then implement any recommendations for enhancement and/or completion that emerge, with an

The Role of the IFIs

IMF/World Bank Update assessment following on later to assess progress.

How effective has this massive programme of work, which has cost well over $1 billion so far, been? That question can, in turn, be broken down into four component parts:

(i) has the exercise enhanced the Fund's ability to identify potential vulnerabilities in the global financial system?

(ii) do market participants value the output and use it, thereby enhancing market disciplines?

(iii) has the FSAP resulted in measurable improvements in the level of compliance with the Standards and Codes in force? And, most importantly,

(iv) is compliance with the Standards and Codes itself associated with more robust financial systems: in other words is all this activity at all worthwhile if the aim is to reduce the incidence of financial crises?

Assessments carried out recently by the Fund and Bank's evaluation staff cast some light on the answers to these questions.[3]

On (i) their conclusion is that the FSAP 'has contributed significantly to assessing financial sector vulnerabilities', though they note some counter-indications. In the Dominican Republic a major financial crisis occurred shortly after the FSAP exercise was completed, and the FSAP did not detect the immediate cause of the crisis. The Fund's work on the financial sector, notably its

---

Box 2   Standards and Codes Relevant for Bank and Fund Work[1/]

Policy Transparency

- **Data Transparency:** the Fund's Special Data Dissemination Standard and General Data Dissemination System (SDDS and GDDS).
- **Fiscal Transparency:** the Fund's Code of Good Practices on Fiscal Transparency.
- **Monetary and Financial Policy Transparency:** the Fund's Code of Good Practices on Transparency in Monetary and Financial Policies (MFPT), (usually assessed under the FSAP).

Financial Sector Regulation and Supervision

- **Banking Supervision:** Basel Committee on Banking Supervision's (BCBS) Core Principles for Effective Banking Supervision (BCP).
- **Securities:** International Organization of Securities Commission's (IOSCO) Objectives and Principles of Securities Regulation.
- **Insurance:** International Association of Insurance Supervisors' (IAIS) Insurance Supervisory Principles (ISP).
- **Payments Systems:** Committee on Payment and Settlements Systems' (CPSS) Core Principles for Systematically Important Payment Systems, complemented by Recommendations for Securities Settlement Systems (RSSS) for countries with significant securities trading.

- **Anti-money Laundering and Combating the Financing of Terrorism**: Financial Action Task Force (FATF)'s 40+9 Recommendations.

Market Integrity

- **Corporate Governance (CG)**: Organization for Economic Cooperation and Development's (OECD) Principles of Corporate Governance.
- **Accounting**: International Accounting Standards Board's (IASB) International Accounting Standards (IAS).
- **Auditing**: International Federation of Accountants' (IFAC) International Standards on Auditing (ISA).
- **Insolvency and Creditor Rights (ICR)**: A standard based on the Bank's Principles for Effective Insolvency and Creditor Rights Systems and the United Nations Commission on International Trade Law (UNCITRAL) Legislative Guide on Insolvency Law.[2]

---

[1] Links to full descriptions of the standards and codes are available at: http://www.fsforum.org/compendium/key_standards_for_sound_financial_system.html

[2] Work is in progress between the Bank and UNCITRAL in consultation with Fund staff to finalize such a standard.

Global Financial Stability reports, has become more thorough and more pointed than before, though it is still criticized for not being rigorous enough in its assessments, or tough enough in its recommendations.

On (ii) their verdict is less positive. The World Bank reports that 'Direct use of the output by market participants remains low, although they may use ROSCs indirectly, through their reliance on rating agencies.' Fifty-five per cent of respondents to a survey said they used ROSCs to some, or to a large extent, though only 10 per cent used them to a large extent, while 21 per cent did not use them at all.

A survey carried out for the evaluation exercise finds very significant differences in the use made by market participants of different codes. On a five-point scale of usage where 1 scores 'not at all' and five scores 'to a very great extent', Basel Core Principles score 3.39 while, at the other extreme, IAIS standards score only 1.42. IOSCO standards are also little valued in the marketplace, with a ranking of 1.70, only half the Basel score. This should cause those organizations to reflect on the rigour and relevance of their standards, and the need to adapt them to changing market conditions and new instruments. Market participants clearly do not find some of them to be of much value at present.

On (iii), whether the exercise has produced measurable improvements in compliance, the evidence is mixed. Survey results indicate that country authorities themselves, on average, thought their participation in the exercise had been very worthwhile, though when asked if it had assisted them in meeting specific regulatory objectives 'they usually thought it did so only to some extent'. It is perhaps to be expected that countries will play down the impact of an external stimulus to change. The Fund believes that the 'evidence points to some implementation of ROSC recommendations' but notes that 'there is neither a mechanism to track systematically members' implementation of ROSC recommendations nor the extent and degree of their observance of the standards in all ROSCs'. Our perception, however, is that FSAPs have often been used in individual countries to bolster the powers and independence of regulators.

Point (iv) is clearly the most important: are the Codes and Standards themselves worthwhile? Is compliance positively correlated with financial stability? It is also by far the most difficult question to answer, and few studies have yet been done on the effect on economic performance of adopting standards. It is also reasonable to point out that some, notably the anti-money laundering standards, have not been introduced for direct economic or market efficiency reasons. They are intended to fight organized crime, corruption and terrorism. The standards in those areas also focus largely on process rather than substance.

Such evidence as there is on this point is hard to interpret. Of six papers prepared on the subject in the IMF, four 'find evidence that adherence to policy transparency and banking supervision standards lowers market spreads, improves ratings, and improves indicators of market performance'. The other two produce weaker, but not contradictory conclusions. On the other hand a study done in the World Bank 'finds no evidence that simply improving supervision has a positive effect on financial sector development, the efficiency of the financial sector, its stability or the corporate governance of banks'. (The conclusions of this study, now published in

book form,[4] are strongly disputed by many regulatory authorities.)

In the light of these lukewarm conclusions, what is the future of the FSAP? The two parallel evaluations recommend its continuation, but in more focused form and with fewer assessments carried out each year. Given the intellectual capital investment made so far that is not a surprising conclusion. The shock to the regulatory system created by the Asian crisis, and the resulting Fund/Bank programmes, may now have diminished. But the International Financial Institutions are unlikely to abandon this area of work lightly, especially at a time when there are question marks over other more traditional dimensions of their missions. And in our view there is sufficient evidence of regulatory upgrades resulting from these efforts to justify the continuation of the programme in some form, albeit with tighter prioritization and within a risk-based framework. We discuss the future content and structure in Chapter 7.

4

The European Union:
A Special Case

Most standard setting and regulatory co-operation at the international level relies on purely voluntary structures. The focus has been on means of exchanging information, on creating rough competitive equality for foreign market entrants or simply on leveraging on other jurisdictions' improvements in supervisory techniques in order to upgrade domestic regimes. However, within the EU, the member states have agreed to bind themselves formally by legislation under the EU treaties to adhere either to similar or, increasingly, identical rules.

Over time an increasingly elaborate structure of legislation has been created, aimed at a diverse and sometimes confusing range of objectives. Alongside this structure have been created, also progressively, a series of intra-European committees aimed at creating common rules, at implementing them in as coherent a fashion as possible, and at engaging in day-to-day co-operation between supervisors. The system is described graphically in Chart 5.

Chart 5 *European Committee Structure*

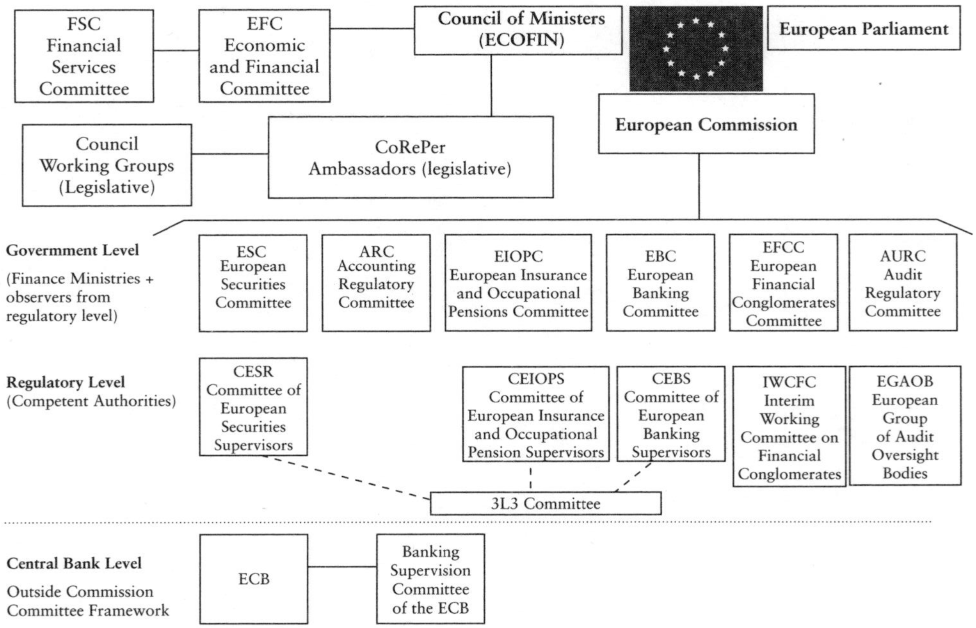

European Parliament

Council of Ministers (ECOFIN)

European Commission

FSC Financial Services Committee

EFC Economic and Financial Committee

CoRePer Ambassadors (legislative)

Council Working Groups (Legislative)

Government Level
(Finance Ministries + observers from regulatory level)

- ESC European Securities Committee
- ARC Accounting Regulatory Committee
- EIOPC European Insurance and Occupational Pensions Committee
- EBC European Banking Committee
- EFCC European Financial Conglomerates Committee
- AURC Audit Regulatory Committee

Regulatory Level
(Competent Authorities)

- CESR Committee of European Securities Supervisors
- CEIOPS Committee of European Insurance and Occupational Pension Supervisors
- CEBS Committee of European Banking Supervisors
- IWCFC Interim Working Committee on Financial Conglomerates
- EGAOB European Group of Audit Oversight Bodies

3L3 Committee

Central Bank Level
Outside Commission Committee Framework

- ECB
- Banking Supervision Committee of the ECB

Source: Adapted with permission from a chart originally devised by John Sloan

The Financial Services Action Plan

The legislative programme has extended over more than fifteen years and is not yet concluded.[1] Its scope has become progressively more ambitious. It started with efforts, by analogy with trade in real goods, to open up the scope for freedom of cross-border establishment of branches and of provision of services from one jurisdiction to another, largely on the basis of mutual recognition of essentially different regulatory regimes. Since then the aims have expanded to include (a) providing a level playing field in relation to solvency requirements, first in banking and securities dealing and soon in insurance, (b) actively promoting the increased provision of particular investment services cross-border, such as mutual funds (known as UCITS) or mortgages through to, much more ambitiously, (c) creating a single capital market for Europe as a whole. Changes have also been needed to amend the structure of rules, once harmonized, to take account of changes in the market.

In some cases the EU has essentially adopted and codified rules created at the global level, as with the Capital Requirements Directive, which gives effect to the Basel II Accord across the EU. In others they have been created from scratch because of the unique circumstances of the EU and the desire to create, insofar as possible, a borderless market.

The impetus for each progressive step has come at different times from different directions. Sometimes, and most frequently, it has come from the larger and more ambitious market participants, frustrated at the obstacles to and cost of expanding their potential cross-border activities.[2] They found that mutual recognition in practice still leaves a double regulatory burden and may well favour the domestic business model as home regulators favour their own firms. Sometimes it has come from business leaders concerned at the risk to European competitiveness and influence arising from the fragmented nature of EU financial markets by comparison to the economies of scale open to financial service providers in the large unitary economies of the US, Japan and potentially China and India. Sometimes it has come from economic and political conviction, as, for instance, expressed in the Lisbon Agenda, agreed at the Heads of Government summit in 2000, that growth in the real economy would be stimulated if the costs of financial intermediation generally were brought down by greater cross-border competition. Quite often it has simply been the product of ideological pressure for greater EU centralization as part of the wider political agenda of ever closer union.

The creation of the Euro produced a powerful additional impetus both because it eliminated exchange rate risk for a vast number of transactions, one important obstacle to cross-border retail business in particular, and because full enjoyment of the wide potential benefits of currency union depends on efficient financial institutions, on deep and liquid capital markets and on sound, cheap and reliable infrastructure. The advent of the Euro, in turn, raised the delicate political question as to whether the focus of the legal framework and of the accompanying supervisory co-operation should be on the Eurozone rather than on the wider EU. The formal legal answer to this question is clear: regulatory directives apply to the EU as a whole. But the pressures for harmonization are stronger within the Eurozone.

The result of this patchwork of motives has been that the precise scope or aims of the programme have rarely been articulated in a coherent framework. The most comprehensive assembly of proposals was the Financial Services Action Plan (FSAP) of 1999,[3] launched by then Commissioner Mario Monti.

This confusingly combined the enhancement and updating of existing prudential rules with a varied array of measures in investment business and capital markets as well as proposals to deal with a variety of technical and legal issues. Measures often found their way onto the list, which totalled no less than forty-two separate initiatives, in part because they served the particular interests of particular groups. There was no agreed overriding vision and certainly little widespread sense or understanding of the likely consequences and wider ramifications of implementation and little cost benefit work. Nevertheless the FSAP involved a shift away from mutual recognition to an approach of proactive pan-European harmonization. It is not clear that the proponents, and especially the UK government, which promoted the FSAP in its presidency and then pushed its completion as part of the Lisbon economic reform agenda, fully understood this shift. The British government saw the FSAP as a market-opening, pro-competition initiative. It was not immediately understood that the single set of rules needed for liberalization and market efficiency, at least for the big players, also implied supranationally integrated supervision.

The overall project turned out to be massively larger, more complex and more resource intensive than anyone had thought and at numerous points influential voices were to be heard wanting to call a halt, either because one or other aspect was going to be vastly more expensive than earlier foreseen or because they found their interests were going to be threatened in ways they had not anticipated. Nevertheless, the Commission pushed doggedly ahead under Commissioner Frits Bolkestein. The project was one of the most grandiose the EU had undertaken, involving change in a vast range of technical and legal requirements across every type of financial institution and activity.

During one of the periods of uncertainty a group of practitioners in the City of London tried retrospectively to make explicit the vision which had implicitly underlain the FSAP. It was never formally adopted by any of the stakeholders, but remains the clearest and most concise statement of the aims implicitly lying behind this massive undertaking.

These practitioners said that they saw the vision as follows:

> . . . an innovative and competitive financial marketplace within which borrowers, issuers of securities and insurance policies, providers of pensions and of financial market services, will interact freely, on a non-discriminatory basis, with lenders, investors and policyholders, and pension plan pur-

chasers. They will do this on the basis of common and pro-portionate prudential regulation and investor or customer protection, on a remote, cross-border basis, if they choose, and have access to all necessary market infrastructures, wherever located, without necessarily requiring a local presence. The market for corporate ownership will safeguard the interests of investors and operate within a framework of sound, proportionate corporate governance and takeover arrangements, and be subject to high quality financial reporting and auditing standards.[4]

Nevertheless, even without an explicit vision, the various measures were slowly put in place in a piecemeal fashion.

It is useful to distinguish between, on the one hand, the prudential projects in banking, insurance and conglomerates – the banking Capital Requirements Directive, the insurance Solvency II project, the Financial Groups Directive for mixed conglomerates – and those aimed at conduct of business in capital markets and investment services. The banking and insurance projects have been described above on (pp. 45 and 76).

Initially the different directives involving investment services were handled separately and the interdependencies between them emerged only slowly. As implementation has yet to take place in many areas it is too early to say whether it will result in the predicted transformational benefits for the non-financial economy. Nor is it possible to say whether only very limited benefit will flow if one particular element is not yet in place or whether there are vital pieces missing altogether from the design whose absence will only become visible in due course.

To achieve full harmonization there need to be unified financial reporting requirements (IFRS Regulation 2002), subject to consistent auditing arrangements (8th Company Law Directive 2006) prepared by companies subject to adequate corporate governance (Corporate Governance Action Plan 2003). The prospectuses they issue need to be in a consistent format and provide consistent information, as well as being accepted across the EU (Prospectus Directive 2003). The primary issuance arrangements need to be standardized and the markets on which the securities are issued need to be consistently regulated (Markets in Financial Instruments Directive (MiFID) 2004). Issuers need subsequently to be subject to consistent continuing obligations to inform the market of emerging developments (Transparency Directive 2004). Secondary trading arrangements need to be consistent (MiFID) and there needs to be common understanding of what constitutes insider trading and market abuse (Market Abuse Directive 2002). Cross-border trading requires reliable and efficient arrangements for clearing and settlement (Settlement Finality Directive 1998, European Code of Conduct on Clearing and Settlement 2006, ECB Target II Securities project launched 2006) and cross-border payments need to be made cheaply and efficiently (Single European Payments Area project, Payments Services Directive 2007). When securities are traded with retail investors consistent conduct of business rules need to apply (MiFID).

The scale of potential change involved in implementing directives for virtually every financial institution and infrastructure provider in the EU is clear. What is not is when or whether they will deliver the benefits hoped for. One of the main imponderables is whether there will be enough standardization of regulatory requirements to facilitate the competition which will generate the increases in efficiency which will benefit final users of financial services. (A further complication is that, even if regulatory standards are standardized, there remain significant legal and tax differences between member states.) The position taken by many at one time was that all that was needed was 'minimum harmonization'. This meant that the basic framework of regulation was to be the same, but that national variation was allowed around it. The benefits of this approach were seen as enabling cherished national features to be preserved where possible. It would also promote competition because variation in national arrangements could facilitate innovation and bring business to the most competitive financial centres.

Those who supported this view opposed 'maximum harmonization'. This meant standardization which, as well as being ideologically pure, promoted the level playing field which all markets need to exist at all, but, if done on the 'wrong' standard, could severely damage competitiveness, especially at the global level, and thwart innovation because of the difficulty in securing changes in legislation (see later on the Lamfalussy processes). Broadly speaking, the proponents of minimum harmonization were the players in the international wholesale markets, mainly in London, while standardization was promoted by those committed philosophically to greater European centralization.

Those positions have shifted over time as it has emerged that the continuing national variation in detail acts, depending on your point of view, as either a barrier to trade or a means of protecting the independence or even very existence of institutions or activities (and hence their respective regulators) in any particular jurisdiction.

Thus the big pan-European firms have increasingly switched from supporting approximate harmonization towards favouring the standardization which enables them to benefit from economies of scale, while some of those earlier committed to centralized standardization as a matter of dogma are beginning to see the threats this inevitably poses to smaller players and marketplaces. (There are other areas where views have shifted – on whether the supervision of the home supervisor should dominate over that over the host and on whether a clear distinction should be made between wholesale and retail business.)

One prime objective was to reduce costs for individual firms by having a single set of rules set by the home supervisor which applied to a firm's operations throughout the EU. These would then be recognized by the host regime and disclosed as necessary to counterparts or customers. The attractions of this approach, particularly promoted by the UK and by large cross-border groups in other EU countries, were evident. However, it became clear that the sheer scale of foreign branches, whether of wholesale firms in centres like London or of large foreign retail operations dominating markets in northern or eastern Europe, has caused a reappraisal of the interests of the host country. (For an account of the scale and nature of cross-border operations in Europe see the ECB's Financial Integration Report 2007.)[5]

At an early stage there was also tension between those who wanted to focus harmonization on the wholesale markets, again typically the UK and large cross-border firms, and to deal with retail separately, if at all, and those other centres, particularly in the Eurozone, for whom the financial services industry was essentially retail-based. Here too views have swung around, with the UK and others beginning to realize, as they came to implementation, that consistency between wholesale and retail approaches was important, just as others began to take in the sheer magnitude of the cost of the changes implied by harmonization at the retail level.

One illustration may help to explain the problem. A notable feature of the changes in the regulation of the capital markets has been abolition with effect from late 2007 of earlier rules at the national level which required all share deals to go through national stock exchanges and makes possible 'systematic internalization' of client orders within investment firms, irrespective of origin. This measure, whose potential significance was recognized at the time, was the subject of bitter debate, but finally agreed, and it is too early to see what the final consequences will be.

Numerous scenarios are possible, each of which may have further ramifications for the structure of supervision, as well as providing great opportunities for some players and problems for others (see Graham Bishop's analysis in 'MiFID – an opportunity to profit').[6] The pressures on established exchanges will certainly encourage more cross-border consolidation, whether simply within Europe, or across the Atlantic or even with Asia, creating the potential for significant economies and cuts in fees, also arising from competition from systematic internalizers (SIs), principally the investment banks. These mergers raise issues for how the regulators of the enlarged exchange groups co-operate and, in the case of mergers with non-EU countries, the extent to which there are pressures for adoption of different regulatory arrangements. (In early 2007 the British government passed legislation to empower the FSA to resist the extraterritorial imposition of US requirements in the event that the London Stock Exchange were acquired by American interests.)

At the same time it is possible, depending on the evolution of other obstacles to trading, that many investment firms will establish systematic internalizers which gain a major share of trading. This business could perhaps become increasingly concentrated in a number of pan-EU SIs, or even global ones, depending on what happens outside the EU, so as to produce, in effect, vertically integrated, global stock exchanges. This would have a serious impact on the traditional exchanges and in time force changes on their own structure or even threaten their viability.

The Commission also continues to work on establishing the extent to which the single market needs harmonized company law and corporate governance arrangements as part of the programme to create an integrated capital market. Their views on this were set out in 2003 in 'Modernising Company Law and Enhancing

Corporate Governance in the European Union – A plan to move forward'.[7] This presented a series of initiatives designed, inter alia, to 'give both issuers and investors the opportunity to be more active on other EU capital markets and to have confidence that the companies they invest in have equivalent corporate governance frameworks'.

The objectives include strengthening shareholders' rights and the protection of third parties, and fostering efficiency and competitiveness of business. The Commission concluded that an EU corporate governance code was not appropriate, essentially because of the diversity of national views, and has instead focused its efforts on enhancing corporate governance disclosure and strengthening shareholders' rights, modernizing the board of directors, capital maintenance and alteration of corporate structures.

Of greater potential significance is the introduction of the European Company Statute (2001), which creates the possibility for companies to migrate between jurisdictions, with consequent implications in the case of a financial services firm for a switch in the identity of home and host regulators, which could be important given the different roles assigned to each. Few companies have yet taken advantage of the statute, although there have recently been some indications of greater interest.

Many of the most intensively developed initiatives have related essentially to wholesale business because this is where cross-border players have been most active and where markets themselves have had a clear need to evolve homogenous arrangements.

Retail provision of services cross-border is far less developed. Bank accounts, personal loans, mortgages, pensions, insurance and investments are still overwhelmingly provided by locally-based firms, whether or not foreign owned. There are many reasons why this is so, quite apart from financial regulation – language, cultural habits, tax arrangements, lack of understanding of or confidence in foreign regulation and redress arrangements, and so on. The case for harmonization of regulation at the retail level is less clear, although this will happen to some extent in any case through the conduct of business provisions of MiFID. Nevertheless, it is arguable that greater cross-border competition at the retail level could still bring benefits for consumers and that more EU-level conduct of business regulation could play a role.

This issue has been subject to extended debate, most recently in the Commission's Green Paper on Retail Financial Services in the Single Market[8] which identifies only modest cross-border activity, wide variations in prices, restricted product diversity and choice, and large variations in market performance. A number of initiatives are proposed in relation to retail banking, mortgage credit, portability of pension rights, cross-border payments, consumer credit, credit information records, distance marketing, etc.

Many of these initiatives remain closer to competition policy rather than traditional financial regulation or involve the creation of new cross-border infrastructure. The logistical challenge of implementing those directives which have already been agreed means that it will be vital to absorb the lessons which have been painfully

learned in terms of the need for thorough 'better regulation' assessment before any further initiatives in the
retail field are undertaken.

Institutional arrangements for co-operation and decision-making

It was recognized in the second half of the 1990s that to
tackle changes on this scale new institutional arrangements were needed. Several problems had to be addressed. The first was that the Commission recognized it
had neither the capacity nor the expertise to draft the legislation unaided. The second was that legislation needed
far more rapid amendment than had been the case in the
past if it was to keep pace with the acceleration of change
in the markets themselves. The third was that the
increased intensity of cross-border business, including
cross-border mergers, required greater co-operation
between supervisors in handling day-to-day business.

A Committee of Wise Men was appointed in July 2001
under the chairmanship of Baron Alexandre Lamfalussy
to make proposals to address these challenges, primarily
in respect of the securities markets where the need
seemed most urgent.

After widespread consultation, Lamfalussy's recommendations[9] the following year were largely adopted. In
future financial services legislation would consist of two
elements. The first, called Level 1, would contain those
basic principles of the legislation which would not need
frequent amendment or which needed high level political

agreement from the EU Council and Parliament. The second, called Level 2, would consist of more detailed, technical features which might need more frequent amendment, perhaps because of market evolution.

It was also recognized that a much larger role was needed for regulators both in terms of providing technical advice on rule-making and in organizing day-to-day co-operation between regulators, including increased convergence in supervisory practice and exchange of information. This activity was designated Level 3, while the process of seeing that legislation was implemented by the Member States and enforced by the Commission (nothing to do with enforcement activity in relation to firms) was called Level 4 (confusingly, since it essentially relates to seeing that levels 1 and 2 work properly).

New committee structures were developed to meet these requirements, in particular to facilitate the provision of detailed technical advice to the Commission on the content of directives and to manage a procedure for fast track amendment through a process known as comitology, which short-circuited the usual political process for agreeing Directives. Committees of member states, usually finance ministries, were established to deal with Level 2 decisions in each sector – the European Securities Committee, European Banking Committee etc. And separate committees of regulators were also established over a period of time.

The establishment of these committees of regulators was reached through a rather tortuous route. Banking supervisors in the EU have for over thirty years met informally at senior level to share experiences, explore best practice in supervisory techniques and, in the margins of their meetings, discuss specific cases. These could cover bilateral issues arising from the cross-border branches or subsidiaries of EU banks or common approaches to banks from non-EU jurisdictions whose supervision or behaviour was problematic or to avoid jurisdictions being picked off one by one.

The informal approach of this 'Groupe de Contact' worked well over many years and, because its discussions had no binding force, it stayed well below the public radar. All this had to change when the new structure of much more detailed legally enforceable directives started to come into being. The creation of more formal structures on the banking side had, in the event, to wait for the rapid emergence of completely fresh institutions on the securities side, driven by the objective of establishing the single capital market and by the explosion of cross-border investment business.

Before the middle of the 1990s the regulators of separate national stock exchanges and capital markets scarcely met each other, with national markets compartmentalized by currency as well as legislation and with regulators seeing themselves more as champions of competing financial centres rather than needing to collaborate. However, with integration gathering pace and as the prospect of the transformation of market structures by the introduction of the Euro grew closer, the national securities commissions in 1997 formed a club for mutual debate – the Forum of European Securities Commissions (FESCO).

As the outline of the programme of legislation became clearer and the list of difficult issues to be resolved exploded, it became clear, as the Lamfalussy Wise Men made plain, that new institutional structures were needed to generate and implement the new kinds of legislation required. At finance ministry level an existing group was transformed into the European Securities Committee (ESC) with a responsibility to give advice to the Commission on high level 'Level 1' legislative proposals and to play a formal role with the Parliament in the decision-making on more detailed Level 2 implementing legislation.

But it was quickly recognized that the bulk of the work had to be done by the regulators through a more formal structure and the Committee of European Securities Regulators (CESR)[10] was created by Commission decision and given its own budget, secretariat and headquarters in Paris. The main committee meets at head of agency level and forms subgroups, either on a standing or permanent basis, to provide advice, after public consultation, to the Commission or to deal with day-to-day co-operation between the regulators, for instance on enforcement.

The creation of this new formal structure on the capital markets side started to raise questions over the suitability of the informal arrangements whereby banking matters were handled through a mixed committee of central bankers and supervisors under the umbrella of the ECB, whose Governing Council claimed supremacy in this area, praying in aid language in the Maastricht Treaty, itself the result of uneasy compromise in an earlier debate over the role of central banks in banking supervision.

The ECB proposed that, if change was needed at all, its Banking Supervision Committee (BSC) should be regarded as the formal counterpart to CESR. However, others argued that this position was unsatisfactory against the background of the new structure on the securities side. Finance ministries considered that independent central banks should not have a formal role in advising on legislation. Non-central bank supervisors believed that non-supervisory central banks should have no formal role in supervisory decision-making. Countries not in the Euro zone argued that the ECB should not have a formal role in the design and execution of policies designed for the single market as a whole. From the point of view of central banks still holding responsibility for banking supervision, the outcome of this debate on supervisory structure at the EU level was thought likely to impinge on their position at a national level.

There was also, however, already a mixed committee of finance ministries, supervisors and central banks. The Banking Advisory Committee (BAC) was formed in 1979 by the First Banking Co-ordination Directive (77/780/EC) and for over twenty years acted as both a comitology and advisory committee.

There was then a hard fought and sometimes bitter debate, the final outcome of which was in 2003 a decision by the Commission, endorsed by governments and the EP[11] that a committee structure analogous to that on the securities side should be created for banking and that this should be replicated also for insurance and pensions, building on the pre-existing Conference of Insurance Supervisors. The Banking Advisory Committee was willing to split itself in two to provide ready made Level 2 and Level 3 committees. Thus were born the Committee of European Banking Supervisors (CEBS) in January 2004,[12] based in London, and the Committee of European Insurance and Occupational Pension Supervisors (CEIOPS) in November 2003,[13] based in Frankfurt. The ECB's Banking Supervision Committee remained in place, but with its focus shifted more clearly to financial stability and to macro-prudential issues. (There is also an Economic and Financial Committee (EFC) which provides the forum for central banks and finance ministries to meet without supervisors and review the wider relationship between the financial system and economy and finance ministers to meet alone in the Financial Services Committee (FSC).)

While CESR has been engaged with the very long and varied list of directives comprising the elements of the single capital market project and in providing MiFID Level 2 advice, CEBS and CEIOPS have been focused on the work needed to introduce risk-based capital requirements, in banking through the implementation of the Basel II project in Europe and in insurance through the creation from scratch of a similarly structured regime for insurance, Solvency (II).

Within CEIOPS the Occupational Pensions Committee has a particular role in implementing the 2004 Directive on the activities and supervision of institutions for occupational retirement supervision (IORP Directive). This Directive creates a framework for the prudential regulation of occupational pension schemes that operate on a funded basis and are outside the scope of social security schemes. It puts in place minimum standards to facilitate cross-border operation by pension schemes. It allows pension funds to manage occupational pension schemes for companies established in another Member

State and allows a pan-European company to have only one pension fund for all its subsidiaries all over Europe. In 2006 the Budapest Protocol set out a formal framework for co-operation in relation to the supervision of institutions that operate cross-border. It remains to be seen whether much use will be made of such cross-border operations and the extent to which the creation of a single market still requires the removal of fiscal and other barriers to the transferability of pension rights.

The need to deal with the challenge posed by the integration of different financial services within single groups also led to the creation of a committee structure to deal both with the formal legal issues arising from the Financial Groups Directive and with practical co-operation in the supervision of the major cross-border cross-discipline financial conglomerates. At ministry level a European Financial Conglomerates Committee was created alongside the other Level 2 committees. No formal cross-sectoral committee has been established at Level 3, partly in deference to potential sensitivity about integrated regulation in national debates about the organization of supervision. Instead, CEBS and CEIOPS have jointly constructed an Interim Working Committee on Financial Conglomerates (IWCFC), with CESR as an observer, to deal with the issues raised by the prudential regulation of mixed conglomerates.[14] The word 'interim' in the title is interesting as this arrangement is explicitly regarded as an interim solution pending the outcome of wide debates on the future of Lamfalussy. Views were divided as to whether it should become a fourth Level 3 committee or remain a co-ordinating mechanism.

147

Clearly, the integration of markets means that the three Level 3 committees need to collaborate on a wide range of issues, and the three committees co-ordinate their activities increasingly intensively through the so-called '3L3' arrangements created through a Joint Protocol in 2005. As well as co-ordinating their work on such issues of substance as outsourcing or reporting requirements, they have also started to work at achieving consistency of process, such as through jointly drawing up guidelines for impact assessment. So far, however, the priorities of the three, and their working methods, have been very different. CESR has been providing Level 2 advice on the implementation of MiFID, while CEIOPS has been working on the principles of Solvency II and CEBS has had the task of sorting out the ramifications of the Capital Requirements Directive.

Chart 5 sets out the broad framework of these committees. But, as with those at the global level, this chart only represents the tip of the iceberg in terms of the structure of sub-committees, expert groups and working parties lying underneath them. At the time of writing in mid 2007 CESR, for instance, had no fewer than nine subgroups. It is not surprising that there is growing pressure from financial firms for simplification.

Financial stability in the EU

The growing cross-border reach of financial institutions in the EU, primarily banks, but also insurance companies, both intertwined through bond and equity markets and their respective derivative markets, has posed questions about what happens if something goes wrong, who is responsible and what tools they have at their disposal.[15] The basic question is which authority is responsible for the different parts of a cross-border group if its solvency comes under threat. For some time it was thought better to leave the answer ambiguous, on the grounds that banks might behave more irresponsibly if it were clear that there were arrangements in place for them to be bailed out, though this may not be a very significant risk if it is clear that amongst the conditions for support will be change of management and loss for shareholders. Acceptance that Europe-wide arrangements to deal with a crisis may be needed, as well as national structures has, however, laid bare a number of challenges to the existing arrangements, based as they are on strict national competence (including for deposit insurance arrangements) for the separate legal entities. (See Goodhart and Schoenmaker.)[16]

Policymakers have been sufficiently concerned at the potential ramifications of a crisis affecting a major cross-border firm that they have played war games at the EU level to try to understand what might be involved. The main problem is that ultimately taxpayers stand behind a bank rescue even if a central bank is the vehicle for providing support. Committing public money to any financial rescue, as happened in the case of Credit Lyonnais or the Nordic banking crises, is a major political issue, and is a decision for finance ministries rather than regulators or central banks. If the bank depositors or creditors are in another country the temperature is raised yet further. The problem is most acute where cross-border branches are concerned. Some are very large and may either form a significant part of the retail financial sector in the host country or be major players in key wholesale markets. In principle, a foreign branch shares in any support given to the head office. Thus the finance ministry in the country of the head office cannot escape bailing out depositors in other countries. Equally, countries where branches are located may face disruption if foreign branches are not rescued, especially if those branches are very large and systematic. Similarly, national deposit insurance schemes may find themselves involved in bailing out, potentially on a substantial scale, depositors in other jurisdictions. The EU Financial Services Committee has been engaged in a debate on burden-sharing in the event of a crisis. The notion that finance ministries might pre-commit to providing some proportion of solvency support is quite unrealistic, but it may be possible to devise contingency plans which would be triggered by a major failure.

These issues are still unresolved, but they raise the question as to whether the point has been reached where some form of supranational crisis resolution arrangements are necessary and, if so, whether a natural counterpart to this is some form of supranational supervisory agency. In any event, there is an issue about whether responsibility and accountability for supervision and responsibility and accountability for financial support need to be aligned. This debate links with the call from some of the large cross-border groups to have a single, or at least a lead supervisor with the ability to co-ordinate the others' work.[17]

Future developments

The European regulatory patchwork, with a plurality of national regimes and sectoral regulators, has led those running the larger groups, most vocally Deutsche Bank,[18] but also a broad coalition within the European Financial Services Round Table,[19] to argue that the regulators themselves should be formally reorganized so that one regulator is responsible for all aspects of a group's supervision across the EU. This model goes beyond the traditional home country consolidated banking supervisor, responsible for ensuring that the group has enough capital and systems and controls sufficiently robust to ensure the head office can indeed manage the group cohesively. The aim is to eliminate the potential and actual conflicts and duplication between a multitude of national and sectoral regulators by entrusting all these responsibilities to a single regulator, either one for each group or conceivably through a single multi-disciplinary regulator for the EU as a whole. (The arguments are usefully summarized in 'The Future of Financial Regulation and Supervision in Europe' by Eddy Wymeersch, the Belgian chair of CESR.)[20]

This model has great attraction as a tool for cutting through the bureaucratic thicket, but there are formidable practical, legal and political obstacles, the most fundamental of which is the misalignment of responsibility and accountability as between the EU 'federal' regulators and the potential claims on national budgets arising from any need to rescue the group financially (see above). As a result, legal and constitutional moves in this direction seem remote. At the same time, the manifest duplication and conflict between national regulators in dealing with a commercially and managerially integrated group bring substantial costs which impose a competitive disadvantage on European firms.

The arguments about the difficulty of allocation of responsibility to provide financial support, and hence liability, do not arise with the same force, however, in relation to conduct of business and a case can more easily be made for a single regulator of investment services activities in the wholesale capital markets, and perhaps particularly in relation to the cross-border infrastructure providers.

As trading venues and post-trade infrastructure providers merge across borders to gain the benefits of common trading platforms and unified rule books, the cost of duplication of regulation of such unified arrangements looks odd and appears directly to undermine the economic aims underlying the creation of the single capital market. Currently such groups are handled through 'colleges' of regulators through which each regulator exercises his national legal powers directly aware of what his peers are doing and ideally in a coordinated fashion. Yet there are still separate reporting systems, duplication of inspections and inconsistency of regulatory requirements. It would be possible to reduce this further, even without legal change, by greater assignment of otherwise duplicative work between national regulators and by creating the presumption that the regulators would act as if unified, with an obligation to explain and justify divergent treatment of arrangements that are identical in the marketplace.

There is also increasing realization that in capital markets more generally the creation of the new legal framework and the desire of market participants to rationalize makes divergence in regulation more difficult to justify, whatever the degree of national discretion formally permitted. For this reason, CESR has led the way, through its formal Peer Review mechanism, in exploring such areas of divergence. There is increasing expectation in the market that regulatory practice should become identical in those areas where the market participants would put in place identical arrangements if they had a free hand. Both CEBS and CEIOPS are now also planning versions of Peer Review.

There are evident tensions here. Just as the heightened competition which the framework is designed to generate will affect the relative profitability of different market participants or infrastructure providers and perhaps threaten their very existence, so the need for regulation will vary over time across national jurisdictions and affect the role of the regulator.

The arrangements for financial regulation face a range of major challenges and a number of issues remain to be resolved. The most fundamental is whether the degree of harmonization achieved between national regulations, still in course of evolution, will in practice deliver the benefits for the users of financial services the single financial market programme was designed to deliver. It is plain that the overall cost of changing the regulatory structure will be very large, even if account could be taken of system upgrading which would have taken place without any FSAP. Furthermore, while legal and tax differences persist regulatory harmonization may not be enough to create a fully efficient single financial market.

This uncertainty about both costs and benefits places a special onus on legislators and regulators to respond intelligently as events unfold, particularly as pressure is placed on cherished national institutions. It is often forgotten that part, at least, of the overall benefits for the economy hoped for from the FSAP derive from driving down costs and hence almost certainly a cut in employment in the less efficient parts of the system.

The other big unresolved issue is how to handle the tensions between the centralization of the management functions at the headquarters of financial groups, the increasing cross-border penetration of banks and insurers and increasing cross-border externalities arising from the potential failure of such groups. There will certainly be continuing pressure to enhance co-operation between home and host authorities. The calls for the appointment of a lead supervisor for prudential supervision of cross-border groups will grow louder and the case for establishing a central agency for prudential supervision of cross-border groups will keep coming back.

5

Regulatory Structures in Individual Countries

One fundamental problem of implementing international agreements in individual countries is the remarkable biodiversity of regulatory systems currently in existence.[1] In this section we review the main characteristics of the different models operated in individual countries, and consider the arguments for and against them.

As the G7 Finance Ministers remain at the apex of the international financial system it is worth beginning there. When looking at suggestions for standardization the Ministers are bound to be influenced by their domestic arrangements.

One simple point is that no two G7 countries have the same structure, as the box shows (Box 3). The overlay of the European superstructures we have just described adds further complexity.

Box 3			
	Insurance	Banking/ deposits	Securities
US	State regulators NAIC	Federal Reserve State regulators OCC FDIC OTS	SEC CFTC NASD and State Securities Regulators and State Attorneys General
UK	FSA	FSA	FSA FRC (accounting and auditing)
Japan	JFSA	JFSA (+BOJ)	JFSA (+SESC)
Germany	BaFin	BaFin (+Buba + LZBs)	BaFin
Italy	ISVAP	Banca d'Italia	CONSOB
Canada	OSFI	OSFI + CDIC	Provincial Securities Commissions
France	CCA	Commission Bancaire (Banque de France)	AMF

The United States

The system of financial regulation in the United States is quite unlike any of the others in the G7. Indeed, it is like

156

no other in the world. Over one hundred different agencies at federal or state level have responsibilities of different kinds. Quite apart from the plethora of regulatory bodies, regulation is also more detailed and intrusive than elsewhere. Insurance regulators, for example, must be consulted on changes in premium rates. There are 1,100 insurance regulators in Texas, almost half the total staff of the FSA, which covers all parts of a much larger financial sector. Bank regulators often carry out detailed assessments of the credit quality of individual loans, a practice scarcely known elsewhere in the developed world. The SEC reviews issue documents at a level of detail unknown elsewhere. As a result, the costs of regulation in the United States are very high. It is difficult to judge whether the benefits justify these costs: most firms think not.

In terms of the institutional structure, there are three principal reasons for its complexity. First, the US financial market is considerably larger than that in any other country. A single regulator for the US financial market, on the UK model, would be an enormous and enormously powerful institution, perhaps too powerful for its own good, and certainly too powerful for Congress. A second reason for complexity is the overlapping jurisdictions of federal and state governments. State governments have been reluctant to cede power to federal agencies, while changes in legislation have increasingly allowed financial institutions themselves to operate on a federal basis. So, in banking, the system which was originally built to handle a banking market where banks took deposits in one state only, now has to cope with interstate banking on a large scale. The third reason for complexity is that is difficult for any administration to implement significant reform. Most legislation in the United States begins in Congress, and there has been no community of interest in Congress in recent years to propose a significant rationalization of regulatory institutions. Rivalry between different Congressional committees does not help. Successive Treasury secretaries have tried and failed to implement fundamental reforms.

Financial institutions themselves are somewhat frustrated by this plethora of regulators with overlapping and sometimes conflicting responsibilities. Successive reports by industry groups have recommended rationalization, if not on the UK model then at least creating some greater simplicity, perhaps by the introduction of a federal insurance regulator, or by the merger of SEC and the CFTC. But while Hank Paulson, as Treasury Secretary, is keen to reform the regulatory system, he has so far focused on the costs and competitiveness disadvantages created by the Sarbanes–Oxley Act as much as on regulatory structure. There seems little likelihood of any fundamental structural reform in the near future, beyond some modest rationalization of the self-regulatory organizations.

Banking and deposit taking

Bank regulation in the US is fragmented. A bank's primary regulator may be the Federal Reserve, the Office of the Controller of the Currency (OCC) (an agency of the US Treasury), the Office of Thrift Supervision (OTS) (another Treasury agency), or one of fifty state banking regulators, depending on the nature of the bank's charter. And within the Federal Reserve system there are twelve districts with twelve different staffing groups, loosely overseen by Board staff in Washington, though with the Reserve Bank of New York playing a central role.

In addition, banks must become members of the Federal Deposit Insurance Corporation (FDIC) which employs 4,500 people to regulate the banks for the purpose of protecting the integrity of its fund, designed to compensate depositors who lose money in the event of the failure of an individual bank. Credit unions are regulated by the National Credit Union Administration.

A full description of the particular responsibilities of each US regulatory entity would be beyond the scope of this book. But the main lines of the system can be sketched out.

The Federal Reserve is responsible for supervising and regulating:

- Bank holding companies, including diversified financial holding companies formed under the Gramm–Leach–Bliley Act of 1999.
- Foreign banks with US operations
- State chartered banks that choose to be members of the Federal Reserve system
- Foreign branches of members, and
- Some other entities such as Edge Act Corporations.

The Office of the Controller of the Currency (OCC) regulates and supervises almost 2,000 National Banks and their subsidiaries. It also supervises federally licensed branches and agencies of foreign banks. National banks are those which are chartered by the OCC. The OCC, established in 1863, has four district offices in the US and a bureau in London. The Controller is also a member of the US representation on the Basel Committee.

The Office of Thrift Supervision (OTS) is the primary regulator of federal savings associations, which include both federal savings banks and federal savings and loans. It replaced the Federal Home Loan Bank Board in 1989, under the Financial Institution Reform, Recovery and Enforcement Act, which was passed by Congress after the savings and loans debacle. The OTS has four regional offices, but no overseas presence, although it considered establishing an office in London to allow it to act as the consolidated supervisor of investment banks containing a thrift – a surprising proposal which the US Treasury aborted.

The National Credit Union Administration supervises federal credit unions and insures savings in those unions through the National Credit Union Share Insurance Fund, the credit union equivalent of the FDIC. The credit union movement is far bigger in the US than in other OECD countries, except Australia and Ireland. There are over 8,000 credit unions in the US with over 80 million members, and assets of around $700 billion.

The Federal Deposit Insurance Corporation (FDIC) fully insures the first $100,000 of deposits in banks and thrifts across the US. It directly supervises over 5,000 institutions, largely state-chartered banks that are not members of the Federal Reserve System. It has six regional offices.

In addition, state chartered banks not members of the Federal System are regulated by state banking departments of varying size and significance. The New York State Banking Department is a large agency, with some international reach: agencies in smaller states are purely local in focus and play no part in international networks.

This diverse system has sometimes been defended on the grounds that competition between agencies promotes efficiency and innovation. In his recent book Alan Greenspan argues that several regulators tend 'to keep one another in check' and that 'the solitary regulator becomes risk averse'.[2] That is hard to prove, and in other contexts the US authorities have argued that regulatory competition can result in the lowering of standards. What is undoubtedly true is that in the case of Basel II US regulators have taken different views internationally and in public, greatly complicating the task of reaching agreed global standards.

Securities

Securities regulation in the US began at state level, and indeed most states still have their own securities commissions, or broader agencies which incorporate a securities regulation function. State-based regulations are, for reasons which even the SEC describes as 'a bit unclear' referred to as 'Blue Sky Laws'.[3] In the 1920s it became apparent that firms could evade these laws by moving offices across state border, which was one of the motivations for the establishment of the SEC in 1933.

For a long period state and federal laws overlapped awkwardly. Much of this overlap was removed by the National Securities Markets Improvement Act 1996, which had the effect of standardizing regulation nationally, and restricting state powers. But issuers and broker dealers must still review each state's particular laws before making issues, or trading. One commentator noted recently that the securities industry continues to be plagued by these overlaps, which 'cause untold delays and inadvertent violations by even the most careful brokerage firm'.

Furthermore, in the aftermath of the collapse of Enron, and other corporate scandals in the US around the turn of the century, a new set of securities regulators appeared on the scene. Perceiving that the SEC's own enquiries were too slow, or perhaps lacking enthusiasm, New York's then Attorney General, Elliot Spitzer (since elected Governor of the State) used Article 23-A of New York State's General Business Law (more commonly known as the Martin Act) to subpoena witnesses and documents and mount investigations into allegations of fraud or illegal activity.

Using these powers, Spitzer sued several large securities firms for inflating stock prices on Initial Public Offerings (IPOs) by giving biased investment advice. The firms concerned paid large fines to settle the case, though without accepting that their advice had been knowingly biased. He then launched further cases into late trading and so-called market timing (which allows privileged clients to trade at prices unavailable to ordinary investors) and contingent commissions in the insurance industry.

Other state securities regulators have taken, or attempted to take similar action, usually with less success. The merits of all these case have been heavily disputed, with the settling firms generally not accepting liability. Whatever the rights and wrongs, which are difficult to disentangle, the episode has added further uncertainty to the regulatory environment.

Although Elliot Spitzer hit the headlines in the early years of the century, the Securities and Exchange Commission remains by a distance the most significant US securities regulator. With eighteen offices and over 3,000 staff it is divided into four main divisions, each with their own distinct approach and culture:

- *Corporation Finance*, which oversees disclosure by public companies
- *Market Regulation*, which oversees the stock exchange and other self-regulatory organizations such as NASD, to which all securities firms must belong
- *Investment Management*, which oversees investment companies and their staff
- *Enforcement*, which investigates violations and brings actions.

Traditionally, the SEC has seen itself as a regulator focused on investor protection. It did not accept the type of responsibility for the financial integrity of the firms in

its sector which would seem natural to a banking supervisor like the Federal Reserve. This approach was
increasingly called into question during the 1990s, as
'broker dealers' (an anachronistic designation the SEC
still uses) like Goldman Sachs and Morgan Stanley grew
rapidly, expanded into new business lines and clearly
became institutions of systemic significance on a global
scale, not least because of the sheer size and complexity
of their own balance sheets. Regulators elsewhere, and
the International Financial Institutions, became inter-
ested in their overall financial health.

A new European law, the Financial Groups Directive,
implemented in 2005, required all firms operating in the
EU to have a consolidated supervisor empowered to
monitor the overall financial integrity of a group, and its
risk controls. For groups headquartered outside Europe,
European supervisors must determine whether they are
subject to equivalent group-wide supervision in their
home country. If not, group supervision must be implemented, at least within Europe, through the establishment of a Europe-wide subsidiary with a ring-fenced
capital base.

The SEC was reluctant to accept this group supervision responsibility: other agencies, notably the OTS,
were surprising candidates to act in the role for the major
investment banks. But the Gramm–Leach–Bliley Act
amended the Securities Exchange Act 1934 to allow an
investment bank to be subject to SEC supervision on a
group basis and to become what is now known as a
Consolidated Supervised Entity (CSE). Since that time,
the SEC has been adapting its policies and procedures

accordingly, though the approaches taken by different parts of the Commission to consolidated supervision still vary markedly.

In all countries other than the US, the same regulator oversees the cash equities and bond markets, and the futures and options markets. In the other country in which futures, options and commodities trading has been long established, the UK, even before the 1997 consolidation, the Securities and Investments Board had responsibility for LIFFE as well as the London Stock Exchange. But as futures and options markets grew in Chicago, on the back of its commodities exchanges, Congress created the Commodities and Futures Trading Commission in 1974. Its legislation was updated by the Commodities and Futures Modification Act 2000.

The CFTC is, at the top, structured on SEC lines, with five Commissioners split on party lines and three principal divisions, of Clearing and Intermediary Oversight, Market Oversight, and Enforcement. Headquartered in Washington, it has four regional offices in Chicago, New York, Kansas City and Minneapolis, alongside the main exchanges. The CFTC is also a member of the Technical Committee of IOSCO, but is not on the US team at the FSF.

There have been regular calls in recent years for a merger of the two Commissions, the logic for which is powerful. Boundary disputes between the two Commissions have regularly broken out. Trading in new instruments has been delayed while the two Commissions contest their jurisdictions and powers. One political obstacle to merger is that the CFTC reports to the Senate

Agriculture Committee, while the SEC reports to the Banking Committee. It is also argued that the SEC is a 'New York' regulator, while the CFTC is a 'Chicago' body – though both are headquartered in Washington, of course.

The Sarbanes–Oxley Act gave the SEC new responsibilities, and also saw the creation of a new regulator, the Public Company Accounting Oversight Board (PCAOB), which depends on the SEC for its statutory authority. The PCAOB conducts reviews of audit quality, and publishes annual summaries of its work on each of the major accounting firms.

Below these federal agencies the New York Stock Exchange has a much broader set of regulatory responsibilities than the London or other European exchanges, and until 2007 the National Association of Securities Dealers was also a powerful regulator. In 2007 the NYSE and NASD merged their regulatory arms, which brought some modest simplification.

Insurance

There is no federal insurance regulator, in spite of several attempts by the Treasury Department and in Congress to create a federal charter, which would allow major companies to be regulated on a national basis. So far, the advocates of state control have continued to resist change effectively.

Each state, therefore, regulates the insurance companies in its jurisdiction. Some Insurance Commissions, in

New York and California for example, are significant organizations. The New York Commission supervises AIG, one of the world's largest financial corporations. Others are tiny, with small staffs and Commissioners appointed with no insurance, or even financial sector, experience whatsoever.

The National Association of Insurance Commissioners, founded as long ago as 1871, attempts to promote harmonization across state boundaries. NAIC aims to act as a forum for the creation of model laws and regulations, but has no power to require their adoption by individual states. The 2004 GAO report into US Financial Regulation[4] notes its weaknesses and points out that it risks falling between two stools, criticized by some for being ineffective in its co-ordinating efforts as a result of reliance on a voluntary approach, yet accused by others of trying to assume too much power over independent state commissions.

In the absence of a federal regulator there is no strong American voice in the International Association of Insurance Supervisors. Nor is there a centre of research and expertise on the financial stability implications of developments in insurance markets. The Boston Fed have attempted to fill the gap with some useful research and publications, but they lack any formal locus.

Canada

Canada's system is an unusual hybrid, with elements of both the UK and US arrangements. Prudential regulation has always been organized on a federal basis, with an Inspector General of Banks appointed in 1925, and an office of insurance regulation established even earlier. Unusually, the Bank of Canada was never given the responsibility for the banking system. The Canadians were also innovators in merging banking and insurance supervision, following the report of the Estey Commission in 1987. The Office of the Superintendent of Financial Institutions (OSFI) was set up at that time, to handle the prudential regulation of banks and insurers. The legislation underpinning OSFI's remit was revised in 1996, and the new legislation was again innovative, particularly with its explicit acknowledgement that preventing the failure of any bank or insurer was not part of the Superintendent's remit. That formulation in turn influenced the draftsmen of the UK's Financial Services and Markets Act, which underpins the FSA.

The deposit protection arrangements, however, are organized on the US model, with a Canadian Deposit Insurance Corporation operating a scheme very similar to the one south of the border, indeed with the same nominal guaranteed deposit of $100,000 Canadian. (An attempt by the government to amend the legislation and remove the duplicative supervision entailed by a separate deposit protection scheme was successfully resisted.)

Securities regulation is handled by the provinces, each of which have Securities Commissions. By far the largest, and the only one of significance internationally, is the Ontario Securities Commission. (Canada is the only major country without a national securities regulator.) They are members of the IOSCO Technical Committee (as, for historical reasons, are the Quebec Commission). The IMF's FSAP in 1999 identified potential problems of co-ordination between Canadian regulators but, overall, gave the system a clean bill of health. Several attempts to achieve consolidation of the provincial securities regulators have come to nothing. Both Quebec, and British Columbia, which has a thriving small company market, are opposed to merger. In 2007 Rodrigo Rato publicly pressed the Canadians to establish a single body, and the Federal Finance Minister declared himself to be in favour of such a move, but provincial resistance remains strong. The Minister has announced a review to examine ways in which a common approach to regulation might be achieved.

Germany

Unlike most other central banks, when it was established after World War 2, the Bundesbank was not given the statutory responsibility for supervision, which rested with an authority in Berlin, known colloquially as the BAKred. Indeed during the debate on the structure of the European Central Bank successive Bundesbank presidents argued that the ECB should not be given any supervision responsibilities, and that they could in some circumstances be incompatible with the monetary policy function.

A parallel body to oversee securities markets, the Federal Securities Supervisory Office (BAWe) was established in Frankfurt in 1995, while insurance regulation was handled by the Federal Insurance Supervisory Office (BAV), created in the 1950s. This superficially tidy three-pillar system was, however, not quite as straightforward as it appeared. In practice, much day-to-day banking supervision was carried out within the Bundesbank system, by the Regional Central Banks (the Landeszentralbanken). And on the securities front, regional governments also continued to play a role. So the front-line regulator of the Frankfurt Stock Exchange (Deutsche Börse) was the Economic Ministry of the Land of Hesse, while the BAWe had exclusive responsibility for international relations with overseas regulators. (This proved a complication when the London and Frankfurt stock exchanges planned to merge in the late 1990s, though the merger failed for other reasons.)

The German government, influenced to some extent by the UK system, concluded that the system was ripe for reform and the Finance Ministry carried out a review, led by State Secretary Caio Koch-Weser, in 2000–1. The then Finance Minister, Hans Eichel, announced the creation of a new unified regulator in January 2001. A storm of protest followed, from the Bundesbank in particular, which now – in the aftermath of the creation of the ECB – took the opposite view to the one it had advanced earlier, maintaining that it would be unwise to separate banking supervision entirely from the central bank. The Bundesbank had itself been preparing a plan to take over the BAKred and integrate its staff with its own. Then President Ernst Welteke led a high-profile campaign in opposition to the government's plans.

The eventual compromise, in 2002, saw the creation of a new authority, the BaFin (Bundesanstalt fur Finanzdiestleistungsaufsicht) but with banking supervision responsibilities shared with the Bundesbank. The BaFin is required to consult the Bundesbank on new rules, and the Bundesbank remains responsible for much of the ongoing monitoring of institutions. The government also failed to resolve the position of the Land governments, who remain responsible for the front-line oversight of exchanges. The overlapping nature of the responsibilities of the two bodies became an issue in 2007 when some Landesbanks were seriously affected by the US subprime crisis. Further changes to the German structure may follow.

While cross-cutting groups have been instituted within the BaFin to handle the supervision of financial conglomerates, and some policy and international functions have been consolidated, the divisions handling the different sectors are institutionally, and in some cases physically separate. The securities regulators remain in Frankfurt, while the banking and insurance staff are now in Bonn (moved from Berlin and Munich as part of a political compromise to compensate Bonn for the shift of most government ministries to Berlin following reunification). This limits the degree of consolidation the new authority can achieve. The BaFin is therefore a less integrated authority than the FSA.

Internationally, the BaFin sits alongside the Bundesbank at the FSF, and also represents Germany at IOSCO and the IAIS.

Italy

Italian regulation follows the traditional three-pillar model, with banking supervision carried out by the Bank of Italy (Banca d'Italia), insurance regulation by the Instituto per la Vigilanza sulle Assicurazioni Private e di Interesse Collettivo (ISVAP) and securities regulation is the responsibility of the Commissione Nazionale per le Società e la Borsa (CONSOB).

As in France, the Italian government reviewed the structure in the early years of the century. The review was complicated by the position of the then Governor, Antonio Fazio, who used his regulatory powers and the Bank's position as the competition authority for the banking sector (an unusual role for a central bank) to resist takeovers of Italian banks. This brought him into conflict with the European Commission.

It seemed possible at one point that the Berlusconi government would strip the Bank of all regulatory responsibilities and create a new entity. But the outcome in 2006 was more modest. Governor Fazio was removed from office, his position weakened by accusations about his personal closeness to heads of individual banks and the receipt of gifts, and replaced by Mario Draghi, a former head of the Italian Treasury official and Goldman Sachs banker with a high international reputation. Competition powers were removed from the Bank, but otherwise responsibilities were left unchanged. The Prodi government, with a former central banker, Tommaso Padoa-Schioppa, as Minister of Finance, seemed unlikely to reduce the central bank's responsibilities further, and there is now some interest in moving to a version of the Dutch 'twin peaks' model (in which the central bank is responsible for all prudential supervision). In 2007 legislation to effect a merger of all the prudential regulators was prepared: it has not yet been implemented.

In international fora both the Banca d'Italia and Consob attend the FSF, Consob is the IOSCO representative, while ISVAP is the Italian member of the IAIS.

France

Regulation in France preserves a distinction between authorization/accreditation and continuing supervision which has long been lost in most other developed countries. So, in banking, the Comité des Établissements de Crédit et des Entreprises d'Investissement (CECE) is responsible for approving new banking licences, while the continuing oversight is carried out by the Banking Commission (Commission Bancaire) which is effectively part of the central bank (Banque de France) and is chaired by the governor. There is, however, a high degree of separation of personnel within the central bank system, and few staff members move between the Commission and the rest of the organization.

The prudential regulation of insurance is the responsibility of the insurance supervision authority (Autorité de controle des assurances et des mutuelles (ACAM), formerly known as the Commission de controle des assurances (CCA)) though, again, a separate committee is formally responsible for authorizing new companies (a relatively rare event in the insurance world).

Following the British reform the French government reconsidered their regulatory structure. While views within government differed, majority opinion favoured a version of the Australian 'twin peaks' model with one body, involving a merger of the Banking and Insurance Commissions, responsible for capital regulation, and another responsible for market conduct. But the Bank of France, concerned not to lose further functions following the loss of monetary policy to the European Central Bank in Frankfurt, resisted the change, which would almost certainly have led to a new Commission outside the Bank.

So only the second 'peak' of the reform was implemented, through the Financial Security Law of 2003, which merged the former Stock Exchange Commission (Commission des Operations de Bourse (COB)) with the smaller Financial Markets Commission (Conseil des Marches Financiers) and the Conseil de Discipline de la Gestion Financière into a new entity entitled the Financial Markets Authority (Autorité des Marchés Financiers). The responsibilities for prudential supervision were left separate. There is now, however, a board of financial authorities, without formal powers, which includes the chairs of the three sectoral bodies.

Internationally, the AMF represents France in IOSCO, the ACAM in IAIS and the Commission Bancaire in Basel. Both the AMF and the Bank of France attend the Financial Stability Forum.

Japan

Until the late 1990s the Ministry of Finance (MOF) had direct control over almost all aspects of financial regulation, though the Bank of Japan also undertook on-site examinations of major financial institutions and the Deposit Insurance Co-operation of Japan (DICJ), established in 1971, administered the deposit insurance system. The DICJ is, however, itself an agency of the MOF. In a sense, the MOF was an early version of an integrated regulator, albeit a highly political one.

During the 1990s this dominance was increasingly criticized, both domestically and internationally. The financial crises which began after the puncturing of the asset price bubble at the beginning of the decade revealed that the MOF had been lax in its oversight of both banks and securities firms. The Ministry's political role, and the unhealthy relationship between officials and the banks – on retirement senior MOF staff were usually found well-paid jobs in the firms they had supervised – were increasingly exposed. A series of costly (to the public purse) rescues were necessary.

Internal MOF reforms, designed to enhance the independence of line supervisors, were deemed inadequate and in 1997 the Government secured Diet approval for the creation of a new supervisory body, known initially as the Financial Supervisory Agency. The JFSA (as it is internationally known) came into existence in June 1998, and was placed under the Prime Minister's office, and headed by a Commissioner with Ministerial rank. In June 2000 the JFSA was reorganized, given powers to draft laws and make rules, and renamed the Financial Services Agency, leaving the English acronym intact. (The Bank of Japan still retains its supervisory responsibilities and pays particular attention to liquidity.)

In international fora, the JFSA represents Japan in the FSF, the Basel Committee (in both cases alongside the Bank of Japan), IOSCO and the IAIS.

United Kingdom

Before the creation of the Financial Services Authority in 1997–8 the UK system was one of the most complex in the world.

Banking supervision was carried out by the Bank of England. The size of the function within the Bank grew rapidly in the late 1980s and early 1990s. During this period there were several awkward episodes: the failure of Johnson Matthey Bank, the closure of BCCI and the subsequent pressure on small banks and, in 1995, the collapse of Barings. The Treasury became increasingly sceptical of the Bank's ability to handle these events, and concerned about the secrecy of its operations. The Treasury believed it had itself been kept in the dark about emerging problems. After the JMB rescue (whose necessity the Treasury disputed after the event) the then Chancellor Nigel Lawson considered removing responsibility from the Bank[5] but eventually settled for the imposition of a new Board of Banking Supervision (BOBS) numerically dominated by outsiders. BOBS, introduced in 1988, sat uncomfortably within the Bank's hierarchy, and its formal powers were limited, though it was used to carry out a review of the supervision of Barings, after the collapse, which led to many important changes in practice which were carried over into the FSA.

Building Societies were supervised separately, by the Building Societies Commission (BSC), part of the Registry of Friendly Societies (RFS), even though recent legislation (the Building Societies Act 1986) had allowed them to compete with banks across practically all of their retail business.

Insurance regulation was handled by a division of the Department of Trade and Industry (DTI), even though the DTI had lost all of its other regulatory functions – while friendly societies (essentially small life insurers) were under the control of the RFS, an untidy arrangement. The Lloyds of London market was largely self-regulated, a situation which was increasingly seen as unsatisfactory by the market itself. It was proving a handicap in overseas markets, especially the United States, where Lloyd's was required to post more capital to back contracts than were domestic insurers.

In securities and investment markets the position was even more complex. The UK clung to a belief in the virtues of self-regulation long after the US and most other developed countries had introduced statutory agencies. A review by Professor Gower in the early 1980s led to the Financial Services Act 1986 which in turn created the Securities and Investments Board (SIB), to conduct statutory oversight and review of a group of self-regulatory organizations (SROs), initially four, later three: the Securities and Futures Authority (SFA), the Investment Management Regulatory Organization (IMRO) and the Personal Investment Authority (PIA). But, ten years on, this two-tier system was widely criticized for the prevalence of turf wars between regulators, and the Maxwell affair and a mis-selling scandal in the personal pensions market had damaged public confidence.

As the 1997 election approached, and a change of government seemed likely, there was widespread expectation of change. Treasury officials made private plans to merge banking and building societies supervision, and to prise insurance regulation out of the DTI prior to setting up a new independent Commission. The SIB drew up a blueprint for a new single securities regulator, which would entail consolidating itself and the SROs into a single tier. Senior Bank of England staff made speeches defending its own role in protecting financial stability. Outside the official sector there were arguments for more radical change. An influential paper by Taylor made the case for two cross-sectoral Commissions, one for prudential regulation and one for conduct of business: the 'twin peaks' proposal.[6]

But the new Labour government's plans proved more dramatic and far-reaching than expected. Two weeks after the election Gordon Brown announced the creation of a new single regulator for essentially the whole of the financial sector, to be chaired by Howard Davies, then Deputy Governor of the Bank of England (and one of the authors of this book), underpinned by a revision of the entire legal basis of financial regulation.

The circumstances in which this reform was announced have been well described elsewhere.[7] The Bank of England's initial reaction was negative, partly because of the speed of change and lack of consultation, but the grant of independence in interest rate policy was quickly seen as the more important gain. The Bank had quietly campaigned for independence for a number of years. There were delicate discussions about the future financial stability role of the Bank, successfully concluded with the signature of a Memorandum of Understanding between the Bank, the Treasury and the FSA in the summer of 1997. Since then, Bank governors have supported the new arrangements.

The reasons for this radical move were never fully explained by the new government. The Chancellor's main interest was the monetary policy reform, which had been carefully prepared in opposition, in considerable detail. Regulatory reform had been given less attention, and it seems clear that the principal driver was the perceived need to make the Bank a 'pure' monetary policy institution (the Bank was stripped of debt management responsibilities at the same time and later of government cash management). The Treasury took the view that the Governor of an independent monetary policy institution, with full responsibility for banking supervision as well, would risk becoming an 'over-mighty citizen'.

Once the decision to remove banking supervision from the Bank was taken, the rest followed more easily. Legislating to set up three new bodies – a Banking Commission, a new single-tier securities regulator and an Insurance Commission, would be cumbersome: far better to acknowledge, and to some extent anticipate, financial sector consolidation by moving in one step to a single Authority.

Market reaction to the announcement was positive, perhaps surprisingly so. That may have been in part a recognition of the fact that a new government, with a large majority, which announced a new policy within weeks of taking office, was bound to have its way. So opposition from the legacy regulators, or regulated firms, was likely to be fruitless. It is generally wise to welcome the inevitable. The Bank of England decided to accept the change, in spite of pressure to campaign against it from overseas central banks, who saw potential implications for their own positions. Supervision staff in the Bank quietly reconciled themselves to the new structure.

The principle of integrated regulation was accepted in Parliament. (The Conservative Opposition did not oppose the Financial Services and Markets Bill at second reading, though the Bill was heavily amended in its passage through Parliament, especially in the House of Lords.) Successive surveys have shown that, while aspects of the FSA's performance have been criticized, international financial firms believe the UK's system is better adapted to the needs of modern financial markets than those of other countries.[8] Recent debates on regulatory improvements in the US have tended to cite the FSA as a model. However, after a decade of smooth operation, the Northern Rock affair in the late summer of 2007 reopened the structural question. Some argued that the

Bank of England's apparent slowness in responding to Northern Rock's liquidity problems reflected communication problems between it and the FSA. The Governor, Mervyn King, defended the tripartite arrangements in Parliament. There will no doubt be a further review.

The general arguments for and against integrated regulation, and on the appropriate role for central banks in banking supervision, are considered below.

China

Given its growing importance in global financial markets, it is worth briefly considering the particular case of China, even though it is not a member of the G7.

Until the reforms of the 1990s practically all financial activity in China took place within, or under the direct authority of the People's Bank of China (PBOC). But over the last fifteen years a number of separate entities have been established, with distinct responsibilities, albeit each with its own close relationship with the PBOC.

The China Securities Regulatory Commission (CSRC) was set up in 1992, to supervise and regulate securities and futures markets. In 1998 the task of supervising companies trading in securities was transferred from the PBOC to the CSRC. At the same time, following the principle that banking, securities and insurance should be separate in China, the China Insurance Regulatory Commission (CIRC) was also established with insurance supervision passed to it from the PBOC.

181

The Chinese authorities showed particular interest in the UK's 1998 reforms, and set a delegation to London in 1999 under the then Deputy Governor, Liu Ming Kang. The report of that mission, widely circulated in China, proved influential in the policy debates which followed, and in 2003 a third separate body was created, the China Banking Regulatory Commission (CBRC), chaired by Liu.

The Chinese leadership have continued to debate regulatory structure, at a series of financial conferences. There are some awkward overlaps between the responsibilities of the three Commissions and the PBOC. They have acknowledged that the system may need to change as the markets develop, and have referred to the possibility of merging the three Commissions in due course. No decision has yet been made.

As of 2007 China remained unrepresented in the key international regulatory committees, though the Hong Kong Monetary Authority attends the FSF, and the Hong Kong Securities and Futures Commission is on the IOSCO Technical Committee. In early 2007 the Trustees of the International Accounting Standards Committee Foundation IASB appointed Zhang Wei-Guo, the Chief Accountant of the CSRC, as a member of the IASB. Other international bodies will need to find ways of bringing China into policy-making functions in the next few years.

Rest of the world

Moving away from the G7 and China, we can find a wide range of different practices. But a rough taxonomy shows that, leaving the United States aside, there are four main models in operation (Chart 6):

1. The traditional three-pillar system, with the central bank overseeing the banks, a securities regulator, usually a separate commission, handling securities markets and an insurance regulator which may or may not still be part of a government ministry.
2. A variety of two-pillar systems, each with their own characteristics. Some (mainly in Latin America) brigade securities and insurance supervision together: others link banking and securities.
3. A so called 'twin peaks' system with one prudential regulator responsible for monitoring capital reserves in all financial institutions, and a second conduct of business regulator with responsibility for transparency and other market or customer transaction-related aspects of regulation, and
4. A single integrated regulator covering all or most of the financial sector in one institution.

There are many different variants of these three models.

In the case of Model 1, there are significant variations in the extent of the central bank's responsibilities, which sometimes cover parts of the securities markets as well. And the dividing line between securities, investment and insurance regulation is set in different places in different countries.

The particular version of Model 2 tends to be influenced by the state of development of the domestic market. In Mexico, for example, securities responsibilities were

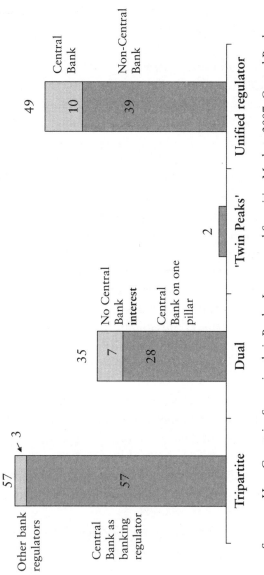

Chart 6   *National Regulatory Structures*

Source: How Countries Supervise their Banks, Insurers and Securities Markets 2007: Central Bank Publications

added to the Banking Commission's remit in 1995. In Colombia the banking superintendent was given responsibility for insurance supervision. It is hard to detect a clear pattern.

Model 3 is also seen in different forms. (There are relatively few examples in operation, though more are under consideration.) The essential feature distinguishing it from Model 2 is that the roles are divided by function, rather than by sector. One agency handles prudential matters, the other information, transparency, market conduct etc. The prudential regulator may or may not be the central bank, and the remit of the conduct of business regulator may be restricted to securities transactions, or may be broader. Australia's prudential regulator is outside the central bank, while the Netherlands regulator is within it, following a merger of De Nederlandsche Bank with the insurance regulator. The Australian reform followed a comprehensive review carried out by the Wallis Commission, whose report carefully argued the case for a separation of prudential and conduct of business regulation.[9]

And even Model 4 can be seen in different forms. For example, integrated regulators may effectively be part of the central bank or monetary authority, as in Ireland or Singapore, or outside it as in Austria or Sweden. They may have total responsibility for supervision of individual institutions, as in the UK, or may share it with the central bank as in Germany and Austria. The regulatory framework may still preserve three legally distinct categories of institution, as in Germany, or it may have a unified approach, as in the UK. And even the most extensive single regulator, with the broadest coverage, may still share responsibilities with other regulatory bodies. In the UK there is, for example, a separate regulator of occupational pensions, and audit, accounting, actuarial and corporate governance regulation is carried out by the Financial Reporting Council, the most complete example of a separate, integrated regulator for corporate reporting.

Moving away from the straightforward question of scope, there are also significant differences in the degree of independence granted to regulatory bodies, both independence from politicians and from financial firms themselves. They may be financed in different ways. And their powers can be differently constructed. Sometimes the regulator can authorize new entities, others simply present a dossier to a committee, or a Ministry, for decision. Some have the responsibility both for regulation, in the sense of rule writing, and for ongoing supervision. Some are prosecutors in their own right, others must pass dossiers to separate prosecution agencies. Some of these differences may well be more significant in terms of the promotion of the financial stability and market integrity than the institutional structure of regulation. We discuss those factors in the next chapter.

6

The Debate on Regulatory Structure

As we showed in Chapter 5 there is great variation in regulatory structures from country to country. Furthermore, the picture across the world is not static. In the last decade many countries have either set up new systems, in the case of transition economies where financial markets themselves have been introduced or reintroduced after a long period of state control, or have reviewed their systems to assess how well suited they are to the changing characters of their markets and subsequently reformed them.

This process of review has produced a widespread, though not universal trend towards regulatory integration. While the first single regulator, properly so called, was created in Norway in 1986, there are now thirty-nine countries who operate along those lines, and the numbers continue to grow (Chart 7). The first 'twin peaks' system was introduced in Australia in 1998.

It is therefore worth assessing the case for regulatory integration in general, and for a single regulator in

Chart 7   *Non-Central Bank Unified Financial Regulators*

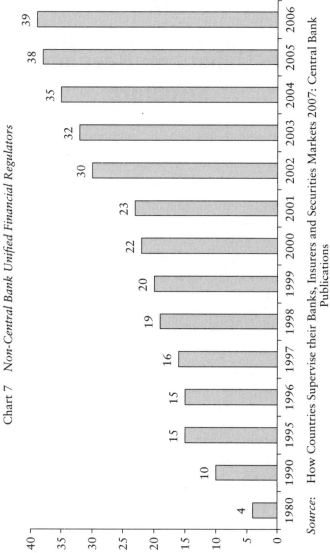

Source: How Countries Supervise their Banks, Insurers and Securities Markets 2007: Central Bank
Publications

particular. (Given the increasing porousness of different sub-sectors of the financial sector, it might be more appropriate to ask what the case for separate sectoral regulators might be, but since they remain the default position, it is still more common to address the question the other way round.)

The case for a single regulator

Although, as described above, the United Kingdom government did not carry out a systematic review of regulatory structure before introducing its 1997 reforms, and has never published a clear summary of the arguments for the FSA, the FSA itself published a paper in 1999 outlining the arguments for its own existence written by Clive Briault, now one of the authority's three managing directors. Briault's paper includes the clearest summary of the case.[1]

He advances six main arguments in favour of a single financial regulator:

1. The growth of financial conglomerates poses a challenge to sector based regulation. The growth in the number of financial conglomerates has been accompanied by a blurring of the boundaries between products, and channels of distribution are no longer as specialized as they once were. It is now difficult to regulate on a functional basis, since a traditional functional approach no longer matches the structure of either firms or markets.

189

2. There is therefore, he argues, a clear need for regulatory oversight of a financial conglomerate as a whole since there may be 'risks arising within the group . . . that are not adequately addressed by any of the specialist prudential supervisory agencies that undertake their work on a solo basis'.[2]

3. While it may be possible to solve this problem through a lead regulator approach, whereby one agency takes responsibility for the co-ordination of the work of others, a single regulator has a number of advantages. In particular:

   a. it ought to be able to generate a number of efficiency gains and

   b. there are economies of scale and scope because a single regulator can introduce a single set of support services, unify statistical reporting, construct a consolidated set of rules and guidance etc. And a firm only needs to deal with one agency, ideally through relationship managers on both sides.

4. In addition to these scale economies, a single regulator ought to be more efficient in the allocation of regulatory resources across both regulated firms and types of regulated activities. A system of risk-based supervision under which resources are devoted to those firms and areas of business which pose the greatest risk is much more effectively undertaken within a single authority.

5. A single regulator ought to be best able to resolve efficiently and effectively the conflicts which inevitably arise between the different objectives of

regulation: notably prudential soundness and consumer protection.

6. A single regulator strengthens accountability. It can be made solely responsible for its performance against statutory objectives, for the regulatory regime, for the costs of regulation and for regulatory failures. (Those who run single regulators may have mixed feelings about this sixth argument from time to time.)

In this, and a further paper published the following year, Briault also addressed some of the counter arguments, particularly those advanced by the advocates of the 'twin peaks' structure, and those who maintain that it is unwise to remove banking supervision from the central bank. These two points require further amplification. They continue to be extensively debated by the staffs of international finance institutions, finance ministries, regulators and of course, central bankers.

'Twin peaks'

The locus classicus of the argument for separating prudential and conduct of business regulation and instituting separate authorities for each is a paper by Michael Taylor, published in 1995: *Twin Peaks: A Regulatory Structure for the New Century*.[3] Taylor also drew on arguments advanced by Charles Goodhart and others.

Taylor argues that the two principal objectives of regulation, systemic protection and consumer protection, are potentially in conflict. He believes that a model which

191

attributes these objectives to different agencies 'institutionalizes the distinction between the systemic protection and consumer protection objectives'. Furthermore, he sees 'profound differences between the style and techniques appropriate to prudential and to conduct of business regulation'. In other speeches and papers, this is sometimes characterized as the difference between the 'doctor' role of the prudential regulator – temperamentally inclined to seek to cure a problem when he finds it, rather than to discipline those who might have been responsible for it – and the 'cop' characteristics of the traditional securities regulator, inclined to reach for the enforcement tool whenever a regulatory breach is seen. This argument is buttressed by the observation that a single regulator 'could potentially become an over mighty bully, a bureaucratic leviathan divorced from the industry it regulates'.

The counter arguments are to some extent inherent in the case for the single regulator outlined above. It may be argued that Taylor and others overdo the distinction between the objectives of systemic and consumer protection. The ultimate argument for financially sound and prudentially well regulated financial institutions is that they are then able to provide financial services and investment opportunities to consumer and businesses which those customers may use with confidence. A breakdown in consumer protection, whether in banking, investment or insurance products, may itself precipitate a wider loss of confidence in types of products or types of firms. There is therefore no necessary conflict between the two aims of regulation. In the long run they are aligned.

Where these aims do cut across each other in the short term, as may sometimes happen (the personal pensions mis-selling scandal in the United Kingdom was perhaps a case in point, where a more aggressive disciplinary approach taken by the SIB or the FSA could have desta-bilized the whole British life insurance industry) there is a need for some reconciliation between the two objec-tives. Goodhart and Taylor argue that it may be prefer-able to resolve conflicts of interest between different objectives at a political level rather than within a single regulator. But there is little evidence in practice that that is so, and it is difficult for a government to intervene effectively and in a timely way, when individual regula-tors have the statutory responsibility to pursue poten-tially conflicting mandates. As Briault argues 'even if all specialist regulators are focused effectively on delivering their own specific mandates, the sum of the parts may not add up to a coherent consistent overall outcome'.

As for the 'over-mighty regulator' argument, the solu-tion may lie more in accountability mechanisms than in regulatory structure. Any regulator, whether sectoral, functional or comprehensively integrated, may act in an over-mighty fashion if it is not subject to appropriate gov-ernance and accountability arrangements. This risk is not significantly greater in the case of a single regulator which may, indeed, need to be more sensitive to market percep-tions of its behaviour because it is potentially exposed to criticism from a wider set of stakeholders.

Perhaps for these reasons, only a small number of countries have found the argument for twin regulators on Taylor lines persuasive. The Wallis Commission in

Australia, which recommended the establishment of the Australian Securities and Investments Commission (ASIC) and the Australian Prudential Regulatory Authority (APRA) followed the prescription quite closely. But the collapse of HIH, Australia's second largest insurance company, in 2001 put the Australian regulatory system under strain. The Royal Commission report on the collapse highlighted some of the difficulties of communication and co-ordination between regulators that resulted from this system, though it stopped short of recommending further structural reform.[4] The only other country to implement what is recognizably a form of 'twin peaks' is the Netherlands, which merged the prudential regulator of insurance companies and pension funds into the central bank, and established a separate financial markets authority alongside it. In that case one of the arguments related to the perceived need to find a continuing role for the central bank, much reduced in status following the loss of its monetary policy responsibilities to the European Central Bank. Similar arguments may, however, now appeal to other central banks finding themselves in the Eurozone.

Central banks and regulation

In most countries, as banking supervision became a more significant function, it grew within the confines of the central bank. There was clearly powerful logic behind this development, particularly when the banking system dominates the financial sector, and when the boundaries between banking, securities and insurance are effectively policed by legislation. The principal arguments for brigading banking supervision alongside monetary policy within the central bank are:

- that there is a powerful relationship between monetary and financial stability. As the then Governor of the Bank of England, Eddie George, said in 1994, 'monetary and financial stability are related. It is inconceivable that the monetary authorities could quietly pursue their stability oriented monetary policy objectives if the financial system through which policy is carried on – and which provides the link with the real economy – were collapsing around their ears.'[5] More recently, Chairman Bernanke of the Federal Reserve has strongly argued for the maintenance of supervision responsibilities within central banks.[6]
- the maturity transformation role of banks makes their failure particularly significant in systemic terms, with a risk of contagion from one institution to another, which justifies the existence of a lender of last resort to intervene in the event of collapse. Since the central bank is the logical lender of last resort, it makes sense for the central bank to undertake supervision. Otherwise, how can it know whether lender of last resort support is justified?

Sometimes other arguments are advanced. For example that central banks have a repository of skills in financial markets and financial regulation which should be used effectively, and that central banks are the agencies with the greatest degree of independence from government, making them better able to operate objectively. These arguments are contingent. There is no reason why skills cannot be transferred from the central bank to another regulator (as was the case in the United Kingdom). The second argument may have some force in developing countries, as discussed below, but it is not now generally relevant elsewhere. And in any case a different form of independence and of accountability is required for a financial regulator.

How valid are the two principal arguments? It is true that the transmission mechanism of monetary policy operates through the financial system. But that does not necessarily mean that the monetary authority needs a close understanding of the financial positions of individual institutions, particularly when reserve requirements are not now used for monetary purposes in most countries. Many aspects of day-to-day banking supervision are well removed from the kind of aggregate information about the financial sector which is involved in reaching monetary policy decisions. As for the second argument, it is no longer so obviously true that banks are the only potentially systemically significant institutions. The failure of Long Term Capital Management, a hedge fund, in 1998 was clearly seen by the Federal Reserve to risk severe systemic consequences. And some of the largest investment 'banks' are still formally constituted as non-bank securities houses. So banks are not as 'special' as they once were. Yet central banks are typically reluctant to extend the assumptions of lender of last resort support to other types of financial institution. If they wish to maintain a role in prudential regulation they may need to rethink that view.

Furthermore, both of these points can be seen as strong arguments for a rich information flow between the banking supervisor and the central bank, but not necessarily for unification of the two. As is the case today with the Bank of England, a central bank can have access to the information it needs about the health of the banking system, either directly from the banks, or through the banking supervisor, even if it does not carry out the supervisory responsibilities themselves.

On the other side of the account, there are arguments against combining monetary policy and supervision. They include:

1. that there might be a conflict of interest which tempts a central bank to loosen its monetary policy stance (or to delay a monetary tightening) because of concerns about the financial health of the banks it regulates;
2. that a loss of credibility arising from perceived regulatory failings may damage the central bank's reputation, and thereby its authority to conduct monetary policy;
3. that the wider the role of a central bank, and the more it takes on regulatory responsibilities which inevitably involve the disposition of property rights, the greater the risk that it will be subject to political pressure or political control, which may undermine the independence of its monetary policy. It is difficult to manage two different types of accountability relationship

with government and parliament within the same institution;[7]

4. there is an argument for the separation of lender of last resort from supervision responsibilities, on the grounds that a lender of last resort which is also responsible for ongoing supervision may be tempted to intervene in support of an institution to cover up the inadequacy of its own supervision. Furthermore, involving two agencies in the decision of whether to rescue an individual institution may improve the quality of decision-making.

How strong are these arguments?

The first point is largely theoretical. As Briault points out, 'there is no firm empirical evidence of the monetary authorities loosening monetary conditions simply in order to support banks or other financial institutions, with the possible exception of the United States in the 1980s. So while there is a risk, it is not one which has frequently crystallized.' Similarly, in an other paper written when at the Bank of England, Briault[8] found no evidence of any impact of either the BCCI or Barings bank failures on the credibility of UK monetary policy as measured by the term structure of inflation expectations – though of course at the time the Bank of England was not statutorily responsible for setting interest rates. He acknowledges that there was some reputational damage, but in the circumstances probably not substantial or long lasting, and not necessarily impinging on monetary policy. Once again, it is a strong argument of principle, though one which is hard to support with practical evidence.

The third and fourth points are, similarly, difficult to 'prove' definitively (as of course are the arguments in favour of unifying monetary and supervision responsibilities).

The authors are in the unusual position of having had responsibilities for banking supervision in both the central bank and integrated regulator. Their observation is that there was little evidence of significant interaction between banking supervisors and monetary policy experts within the Bank of England when it combined the two functions. Indeed the staffing and skill needs of the two sections of the Bank had been drifting apart for some years, as a higher degree of professionalism was required in both functions, as each became more technical and more complex. In practice, there were far more interactions between banking supervisors and the separate regulators of other parts of the financial sector, than there were between banking supervisors and monetary policy staff within the Bank of England. This empirical observation may, in the authors' view, be as important as some of the theoretical arguments described above. In the event of a crisis, and in those unusual circumstances where there may be some trade off between monetary and financial stability, good communication is vital. But it is not axiomatic that that requires the two functions to be held within a single institution.

They also note that, in practice, the Memorandum of Understanding agreed between the Treasury, the Bank of England and the FSA has worked smoothly for a number of years, and the Bank of England has not in practice felt itself to be deprived of information about the financial sector which it needs for its other functions. Furthermore, it is arguable that the Bank can now take a broader view of financial sector developments than it could when it was directly responsible for banking supervision, but had no structural relationship with regulators of other parts of the financial sector. Certainly, the arrangements for the flow of information are far more systematic and comprehensive than they were. The cross-membership arrangement between the Bank of England's Court of Governors, and the FSA's Board, helps with effective communication between the two authorities, though the key factor is the maintenance of good working relationships between the staff of the two institutions. That communication, through an open legal gateway, covers information affecting securities markets and insurance companies and investment funds, as well as banks. In recent years, some of the most worrying financial developments, with potential implications for financial stability and perhaps for economic behaviour and hence monetary policy, have occurred in those sectors. It is, however, absolutely essential that the two organizations liaise very closely, and reach a common view on how to react to emerging problems very rapidly. The post-mortems following the Northern Rock problem will focus on whether this communication and liaison was effective in practice.

International practice shows that there is, as yet, no emerging consensus on this issue. The number of single regulators continues to grow, though some are within central banks. The range of practice on the role of central banks in regulation is highly diverse (Chart 8). Of a

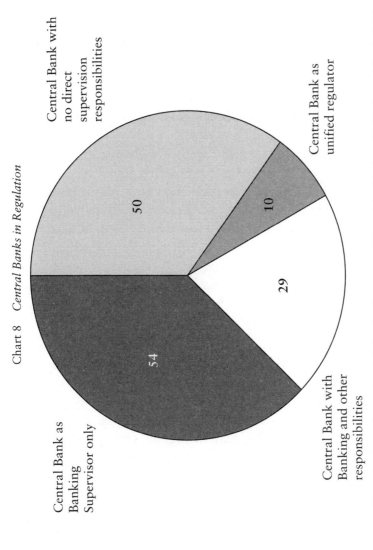

Chart 8 *Central Banks in Regulation*

Central Bank with no direct supervision responsibilities

Central Bank as unified regulator

Central Bank as Banking Supervisor only

Central Bank with Banking and other responsibilities

50

10

54

29

Source: How Countries Supervise their Banks, Insurers and Securities Markets 2007: Central Bank Publications

sample of 143 countries, in fifty of them the central bank has no supervisory responsibilities, and in a further twenty-nine it shares banking supervision responsibilities with another agency, while in sixty-four countries it has the prime responsibility.

Choosing the best regulatory structure

These arguments, taken together, perhaps explain why there have been moves towards integrated regulation around the world. But each country needs to make a careful assessment of its own position. Llewellyn[9] provides a catalogue of the factors which countries need to take into consideration as they make the structural choice (Box 4).

Box 4   Issues to Consider in Determining Regulatory Structure

- What is the appropriate number of regulatory agencies and, in particular, should there be a series of specialist regulators, integrated agencies responsible for more than one sector of the financial system, or a single, all-embracing agency responsible for all aspects of regulation in the financial system?
- Should prudential and conduct-of-business regulation be separated or combined within a single agency?

- What role should the central bank have in the regulatory and supervisory process?
- If there is no single regulator, what structure of agencies is most appropriate, which functions and firms should be allocated to which agencies, and how should the objectives for each agency be defined? In particular, how should *functional* and *institutional* dimensions of regulation be allocated among agencies?
- What specific objectives should each regulatory and supervisory agency have?
- What degree of co-ordination is required between different agencies, and what mechanisms are needed to ensure effective co-ordination, co-operation, and information sharing?
- What degree of political independence should regulatory and supervisory agencies have?
- Insofar as regulation has consequences for competition, what role, if any, is there for competition authorities in the regulatory process?
- To what extent is concentration of power an issue to consider in establishing the optimal institutional structure?
- What role, if any, should be given to self-regulation and mechanisms for practitioner input?
- What institutional mechanisms are most efficient at facilitating international co-ordination and co-operation between national regulatory agencies?
- How much independence and accountability should regulatory agencies have?

It is certainly necessary to consider the extent to which the financial sector is integrated. Where there are statutory barriers to cross-sectoral activity, the arguments for regulatory integration are significantly weaker. And the institutional independence point is certainly crucial. There are countries at an immature stage of political development, or where an individual or a group of individuals is excessively dominant, where it is unrealistic to think that a new independent agency, with the market power of a single financial regulator, could be created with the appropriate accountability framework and checks and balances built around it. In those circumstances, while the central bank may be an imperfect solution, it may be the best available. In most other countries, the arguments for regulatory integration look more powerful. The US is, of course, a long way from such consolidation, and powerful voices, including Alan Greenspan's, have argued against it.

How strong are the arguments for regulatory competition within one country? In our view, they are weak. In the first place, there is cross-border competition, which brings some of the benefits adduced. Secondly, there is little or no evidence that competition has brought enhanced efficiency. US regulatory bodies are very generously staffed by international standards. Third, because of the risk of a 'race to the bottom' regulatory competition is in any case heavily constrained by legislation.

It is difficult to avoid the conclusion that the argument is more a partial retrospective justification of complexity than a principle on which a regulatory system should be built.

Debate on Regulatory Structure

Does regulatory structure matter?

As Llewellyn points out, there are question marks about the extent to which regulatory structure is in itself any guarantee of financial stability, or of the economic efficiency of a country's financial markets. There is little solid evidence on this point. Indeed such evidence as there is on the relationship between regulatory arrangements and credibility and financial stability tend to relate to the characteristics of those agencies in terms of corporate governance and independence, rather than to their institutional structure in itself.

Some researchers have found statistically significant relationships confirming the importance of good regulatory governance for the soundness of the financial system, by constructing indices of financial stability and sound corporate governance within regulatory agencies for a large sample of countries.[10] An IMF paper notes that the independence and accountability of regulators have been increasing, and that both characteristics are positive for financial stability.[11] More recent research by Steve Donzé at the LSE (so far unpublished) suggests a strong relationship between regulatory independence and financial stability. Donzé has constructed an index of independence, covering both independence from political control on the one hand, and from market participants on the other. This research suggests that independence and integrity are more important than structure – not in itself a surprising result – as far as big issues of avoidance of financial crises are concerned.

But three further points may be made in this connection:

1. The avoidance of financial crisis and financial instability is not the only purpose of regulation. There is evidence that confident and competent regulators deliver other types of economic benefit by increasing confidence in financial intermediation and reducing risk premia.
2. While there is no necessary relationship between structure and independence, countries which have reformed their regulatory structures have often taken advantage of that reform process to enhance the independence of the bodies involved, and
3. From the point of view of the competitiveness and degree of competition in financial markets the views of market participants on the regulatory regime are also relevant. Successive surveys have shown that firms themselves believe that the London regime, with its integrated regulator, is better suited to today's financial markets, and is likely to out-perform other regulatory regimes, based on sectoral approaches, in the future.

Rules versus principles

In the last two or three years there has been mounting concern in the US, in particular, about the impact of increasingly detailed rules on the dynamism and flexibility of financial markets. That concern was focused on

206

the SEC, in particular, and on the implications of the Sarbanes–Oxley Act. Those concerns have been accentuated by evidence that financial business has been switched from New York to London, and firms have argued that one reason for this switch is the more flexible principles-based regime operated by the Financial Services Authority. This point emerged in a number of reports on the subject, notably in that prepared by McKinsey and Company for the City of New York.[12]

How real is the distinction in practice? How far is it true that the UK regime is principle based, and is a principle based regime in all respects to be preferred to one based on black letter rules?

It is certainly true that the capstone of the FSA regime is a set of regulatory principles, couched in straightforward language (see Box 5). Those principles were, in fact, inherited from the Securities and Investments Board, but adapted for use across all financial businesses.

A set of agreed principles certainly allows the possibility of a simpler rulebook, in that it is not necessary in most circumstances to define with precision every type of behaviour which the regulator would regard as incompatible with its regime. That is only true, however, if the principles themselves can be used as the basis for enforcement action, without the regulator needing to specify a particular rule breach. Many market participants have sought to resist that interpretation of the status of the principles, but without it a principles-based regime means little. The FSA has, therefore, always made it clear that it will enforce on the basis of principles alone, and has done so on several occasions.

Box 5   The FSA Principles

1. Integrity
A firm must conduct its business with integrity.

2. Skill, Care and Diligence
A firm must conduct its business with due skill, care and diligence.

3. Management and Control
A firm must take reasonable care to organize and control its affairs responsibly and effectively, with adequate risk management systems.

4. Financial Prudence
A firm must maintain adequate financial resources.

5. Market Conduct
A firm must observe proper standards of market conduct.

6. Customers' Interest
A firm must pay due regard to the interests of its customers and treat them fairly.

7. Communications with Customers
A firm must pay due regard to the information needs of its clients and communicate information to them in a way which is clear, fair and not misleading.

8. Conflicts of Interest
A firm must manage conflicts of interest fairly, both between itself and its customers and between a customer and another client.

9. Customers: Relationship of Trust
A firm must take reasonable care to ensure the suitability of its advice and discretionary decisions for any customer who is entitled to rely upon its judgement.

10. Customers' Assets
A firm must arrange adequate protection for clients' assets when it is responsible for them.

11. Relations with Regulators
A firm must deal with its regulators in an open and co-operative way, and must disclose to the FSA appropriately anything relating to the firm of which the FSA would reasonably expect notice.

A principles-based approach is not so starkly different from rule-based regulation as it may appear. Anyone who has studied the FSA Handbook will note that it is a very extensive document indeed. In part, that results from pressure from the market itself, and especially from lawyers. During the process of articulating the new regime in the UK the consultations with the market typically resulted in more extensive rules and guidance, as firms and their lawyers pressed for greater certainty about behaviours which the regulator would find acceptable and unacceptable. So we are talking here about a spectrum, rather than a binary question of rules or principles. A set of agreed principles can allow some rule-book simplification and provide the regulator with the needed flexibility to respond to market developments quickly. It can also provide some greater flexibility for firms themselves. But it is not a substitute for a good understanding between regulators and regulated about what is and is not acceptable market practice, and it can only work effectively if individual supervisors are trained to make judgements and feel confident in so doing. Principles-based approaches are likely to require up-skilling of regulators, and probably, over time, fewer, better rewarded staff.

Self-regulation

There is also a continuing debate about how far it is appropriate, and indeed preferable to rely on self-regulatory mechanisms in financial markets, as an alternative to statutory regulation.

The proponents of self-regulation argue that it is likely to be more market sensitive and more flexible. Regulations will be designed by people more familiar with market practices than are the lawyers and officers working for state regulatory bodies. Where regulations are drawn up and agreed by market practitioners there is likely to be more wholehearted 'buy in' on the part of those practitioners, which should result in better compliance with them. As for enforcement, attracting the public opprobrium of one's peers may be a more feared penalty than a fine imposed by an organ of the state, where many other market participants may be sceptical about its appropriateness or validity. There is some evidence that market participants can be strict with colleagues who break 'club rules', sometimes tougher than statutory regulators might be. Also, discipline imposed by self-regulators can be faster, with less scope for lengthy appeals.

On the other hand, sceptics of self-regulation point to a chequered experience in a number of countries, notably the UK. There are difficulties in ensuring comprehensive coverage of self-regulatory regimes. Seeking to require all firms of a particular sort to register with a self-regulator may be contrary to competition law. Further, self-regulators, while they may be effective in dealing with the 'bad apple in the barrel', have more difficulty in promoting regulatory changes which raise standards of market behaviour. And they depend for their authority on a perception among the members that they have a common interest in each other's reputations. When different sub-sectors of financial markets were easily identifiable as the preserve of particular types of firm, that was a sound basis for self-regulatory discipline. Now, with the breakdown of barriers of different sectors of financial markets in many countries, there is much less common identity in those sectors.

It is not possible to 'score' this debate in one way, for all time and in all places. It is also important to note that self-regulation can mean different things in different countries, in different markets. International debate has been somewhat confused for that reason. A very simple taxonomy of self-regulation suggests four distinct, albeit potentially overlapping models:

1. Pure self-regulation, in which market participants draw up the rules and police them with no statutory backing or government involvement in the process.

2. Self-regulatory organizations which are largely responsible for their own regimes, but where there is a process of statutory recognition of their rules as standards and codes for the sector as a whole, and therefore statutory backup for enforcement.
3. Self-regulation which sits on top of a statutory regime, perhaps adding additional standards of ethical behaviour and customer service to the requirements of statutory regulation.
4. Practitioner involvement in the development of statutory regimes, whether through consultation or some formal locus in the process.

The UK regime has moved along this spectrum over the last twenty years. Before the Financial Services Act 1986 the market was largely self-regulated under a form of Model 1. The 1986 Act introduced statutory backing for the self-regulators and a statutory regulator to oversee them, while the Financial Services and Markets Act 2001 abolished the previous Self-Regulatory Organizations (SROs) in favour of a single tier of statutory regulation. But that tier was developed with extensive practitioner involvement (Model 4) with practitioners on the decision-making board of the FSA. And there remains room for super-equivalent provisions devised by bodies such as the Securities Institute or the Banking Code Compliance Board, which are not appointed by or directed by the government or the FSA. The FSA has, however, resisted giving statutory backing to codes devised by purely self-regulatory bodies.

While SROs continue to play an important role in

some countries, notably the US where the role of the NASD, in particular, is important, and in the accounting and auditing area more generally, there has been a general if not universal trend towards statute-based regulation in recent years. That trend seems likely to continue. In addition to the concerns about the effectiveness of SROs, described above, there is one additional point which has assumed increasing importance. Where regulators operate systems of mutual recognition, and allow firms to operate in their jurisdictions on the basis of regulatory standards imposed or maintained elsewhere, statutory regulation is evidently preferable and may be required. It is difficult for a regulator in country A to agree to place legal reliance on a regime of self-regulation in country B. That is especially true in the European Union, where SROs are rarely able to meet the exacting standards and comprehensive coverage set in European directives and it is also likely to be the case as the US and other countries start to move towards mutual reliance.

However, this somewhat pessimistic verdict on self-regulation should not be read as devaluing the importance of a close dialogue between the regulators and the regulated. To remain up to speed with market developments regulatory authorities need to maintain close links with firms and their representative bodies. The FSA uses a formal mechanism – the Practitioner Panel – for this purpose. Where they do not have one, other regulators should consider a similar approach.

7

The Need for Reform

How robust is the international system of regulation we have described? It looks extremely cumbersome, involving complex structures intersecting at many levels and locations. It is clear that, if we were starting afresh, we would not create the system we now have, with all its overlaps, underlaps and complexity. We acknowledge that the system has operated tolerably well in recent years. Even though the structures look Byzantine, habits of collaboration between institutions, and individuals within them, assisted by the fact that the whole system operates entirely in English, are such that information flows quickly between countries when necessary. But the overall economic environment has until recently been remarkably benign during the recent extensive period of further internationalization of the financial system. And the market turbulence which began in the summer of 2007 has once again highlighted the weaknesses, and the lack of strong mechanisms of crisis management which respond to the growing interconnectedness of markets and involve important new actors, such as the Chinese.

One obvious response, which has already been advocated, is to strengthen the powers of the International Financial Institutions, or indeed create a new World Financial Authority. Our view, by contrast, is that it is not currently realistic to argue for the pooling of sovereignty in this area. There is no evidence, except perhaps in the special case of the European Union, that governments are willing to cede authority over their domestic financial systems to regulators overseas. It may be some time before further shifts in that direction become a realistic option. And movement will almost certainly not come until there is a malfunction which generates a political imperative for reform.

Nonetheless, there are a number of weaknesses in the existing arrangements, which ought to be addressed. In this chapter we propose a series of reforms which would increase the resilience of the system.

Simplification

The charts in Chapter 1 vividly illustrate the complexity of the existing arrangements. Year-by-year new committees and working groups are added: few ever die. The number of groups in which the FSA is represented has more than doubled in the last decade.

There is not scope here to produce a detailed list of candidates for the regulatory morgue, though we make some suggestions below. Conducting a fundamental review with a view to eliminating redundant groupings and amalgamating overlapping bodies would be a useful function for a strengthened FSF. The G7 Finance Ministers should ask the FSF to undertake it.

One underlying reason for the complexity is the persistence of very diverse regulatory systems in individual countries. Many still operate sectoral arrangements, even where they allow universal banking, and cross-ownership of banks and insurers. Regulatory reform at home would facilitate international rationalization. That is especially true in the European Union, where the existence of three separate committees, each with its own premises and staff in different cities, is impossible to justify on any rational basis. Those countries which have not recently reviewed the appropriateness of their structures, in the light of market developments, should do so, perhaps using the taxonomy in Chapter 6. Specifically, they should ask themselves whether their regulators are able to interface effectively with the key international groupings.

Co-location of the international regulators at the BIS in Basel, where two are already established, would help, as would co-location of the three EU Committees in Brussels, with a common secretariat.

Legitimacy

For the system to work effectively, and for the agreements on standards and codes reached by international groups to be accepted and implemented worldwide, the bodies and committees themselves must be thought to have an adequate degree of legitimacy, which is likely to be maximized if they are seen to be properly representative of different parts of the world and of countries at different stages of financial development. As can be seen from the descriptions in Chapter 2 the existing networks vary greatly in their composition and representativeness. In some cases their composition is clearly in need of revision, and reflects an out of date view of the balance of power in the global financial system.

This is most obviously the case in relation to the Basel Committee. Of the thirteen members, ten are from Europe, including Belgium, Luxembourg and Sweden. The only member from Asia is Japan and there is no member at all from the southern hemisphere. Curiously, the most recent expansion of the group saw the addition of yet another European country, Spain. And European domination of the Committee is further accentuated by the presence at the meetings of both the European Commission and the European Central Bank, even though the latter has no banking supervision responsibilities.

This composition can surely not survive much longer if the Basel Committee's role is to be sustained at the centre of the banking system. Of course, there is a trade off between committee size and effectiveness. Undoubtedly a Committee of thirteen countries has a greater chance of achieving consensus than a much larger and more diverse group (though it is hard to see that Basel II could have taken much longer than it did).

This argues for some reduction in European membership, to allow the addition of other countries. Some
progress has been made in engaging other supervisors
through the International Liaison Group and through
the sub-committees of the Accord Implementation
Group, but the logic of the Basel Committee composition is that, since the Committee sets rules for cross-
border banks, its members should be from the those
countries which are the domiciles of internationally
active banks. That now points to the addition of China,
certainly, whose banking system accounts for some 9 per
cent of the world total and whose banks are increasingly
active internationally, and probably Australia, several of
whose banks are very active overseas. There will also be
a case for adding both India and Singapore in due course,
and it is likely that other countries will find themselves
with major international banks in the next decade. Some
of the smaller European countries should leave, to
prevent the Committee becoming unwieldy. This reform
of the composition of the Basel Committee is long
overdue.

There is a question mark, too, about the Committee's
accountability. At present, it reports to the G10
Governors (in practice a group of thirteen). Yet, now,
eight of these thirteen governors have either no responsibility for banking supervision in their jurisdictions, or
only a supporting role, as in the case of the German
Bundesbank. In response to this curiosity, the governors now convene, on an informal basis, a group of
governors and heads of supervision, but this is only an
advisory body, and has no official status. It does not

select the committee's chair, for example. The governors have guarded their overall control of the Basel Committee carefully, and have so far always insisted that the chair of the Committee should be a Central Bank governor, even though it is increasingly difficult to field Central Bank governors with appropriate experience and domestic responsibilities. Indeed this was the main reason for the addition of Spain to the Committee in 2001, in order to provide a governor with supervision expertise who was in a position to take over the chair. So, in addition to a change in membership, the Basel Committee needs a different accountability structure, which fully incorporates the heads of financial supervision in the major countries represented on it.

The problems of legitimacy are somewhat less acute in the case of both IOSCO and the IAIS. They already have broader, indeed comprehensive membership, and there are democratic procedures within them. But, in the case of IOSCO, democracy extends to the Executive Committee, but not to the Technical Committee which is the key forum in which standards are set. And that Committee is also rather strange in its construction, with two Canadian members, for example, yet no permanent representatives from China or India, which have growing and increasingly dynamic equity markets. So reform is needed in those cases, too.

The issues are rather different in relation to accounting and auditing, where the standard setters have never been representatives of national regulators. The focus so far has rather been on the more fundamental question of removing standard setting decisions from those being regulated.

While the creation of the IASB under the auspices of the IASC Foundation has shifted responsibility for creating international accounting standards from the accounting profession, this is not yet the case for auditing standards, which remain formally determined by the auditing profession, albeit with some discipline generated by voluntary adherence to the procedural requirements of the Public Interest Oversight Board. It seems odd that, while there are now independent public audit oversight bodies, standard setting remains the province of the regulated, by contrast to the arrangements in other fields of financial regulation. This should be changed so that international audit standards are set by an independent public board, an International Board for Audit Standards, perhaps analogous to the IASB arrangements, once residual concerns about the funding and accountability of the IASB are resolved. These come back to the extent to which sovereign states are willing to relinquish individual representation in standard setting in the interest of effective and efficient collective decision-taking. At the very least, funding of the standard setters should be provided through the budgets of the national authorities responsible for accounting and audit regulation rather than from the current unsatisfactory ad-hoc group of accounting firms and corporations. It would then be possible to put the audit, accountancy and, in due course, actuarial standard-setters within a single overarching framework, perhaps by extending the remit of a reformed IASC foundation.

At the apex of the system, the Financial Stability Forum has tentatively extended its membership beyond the G7. Given the tripartite membership from each G7 country (which in due course should be reviewed), there is clearly more of a risk in the case of the FSF of dilution and ineffectiveness if a number of other countries are added. But, over time, it will need to broaden its membership to include representatives from major new financial centres. It is reasonable, for a body which is focusing on financial stability, and on the interaction between markets, that its membership should be drawn predominantly from countries whose markets are international in character, and where developments in those markets can influence others. So sheer size of the domestic economy is not necessarily the appropriate criterion. It seems probable, however, that Shanghai, and perhaps Mumbai, will become significant global financial centres in the reasonably near future. So China and India should soon be added, and the Netherlands and Italy dropped.

Structure

The global regulatory architecture is clearly driven by the former dominance of the three pillar system. As we have shown, this model of domestic organization is now by no means universal, and the number of integrated regulators has been growing steadily. But the international groupings largely reflect the national position at the time they were created in the 1980s and 1990s. The only significant change which resulted from analysis of the causes of the Asian financial crisis, was the establishment of the Financial Stability Forum in 1999.

Are these structures still adequate to cope with the challenges of financial stability, or is a fundamental reorganization of the international financial architecture necessary?

The authors' preferences on this point are clear. We believe that in increasingly sophisticated financial markets the old three pillar system is no longer appropriate. Were more national authorities to be reorganized on unified lines, then the logic of restructuring the global bodies would be very powerful. The main issues which international regulators now face are not easily soluble in any one of the existing Committees acting alone. Many of the challenges to financial stability now come from institutions which do not fit neatly into the definitions we typically use: private equity and hedge funds are a complex mix of intermediary and principal. Their activities are fuelled by credit provided by the banking system, yet they operate largely in traded markets, both regulated and unregulated. They are invested in by insurance and pension funds. It is most unlikely that any future crisis will be confined to a single regulated sector.

But radical change will not be easy to introduce, and there is no current sign that a new consensus on the international architecture is emerging. In the short to medium term, therefore, the best answer would be to strengthen the Financial Stability Forum, and to make it a more influential body. There are several useful changes which could be made:

The Need for Reform

a. The Forum could be renamed the Financial Stability Council. This would signal that the G7 Finance Ministers saw it as a more important entity, and one which was capable of making its own decisions, rather than simply acting as a clearing house for initiatives and ideas emerging elsewhere. It should also be given enhanced resources, by the BIS or its members, or both. It should formalize its power to commission work from others and be given the necessary authority to follow up on the outputs of such work.

b. The Forum/Council should go back to the practice it introduced at its early meetings, and commission work of its own, in areas where there are cross sectoral issues, or broad financial stability questions to address which arise out of the changed structure of global intermediation. In this context it is encouraging that, when they wished to reconsider the role of hedge funds in the international financial system, the G7 Finance Ministers in early 2007 asked the Financial Stability Forum to revisit its work on highly leveraged institutions in 2000. Since publishing its first three reports on HLIs, international capital flows and offshore centres, the Forum has typically looked elsewhere for its input. That was as a result of American resistance to self-generated work. That resistance should be resisted, and the Forum should take its own initiatives where the case to do so is made out. A renewed initiative to seek to address how to resolve cross-border insolvencies would be highly desirable before the system is tested again by much more complex deals than existed in the past. Another issue of cross-cutting concern which the FSF could usefully address is the risks to financial stability arising from concentration in the global audit market and from the absence of consolidated oversight over the global networks of audit firms.

c. The Secretariat should be strengthened. There is no need to move it physically from the BIS, although the links which need to be particularly reinforced are those between the FSF and the IMF and the World Bank, so it also needs a presence in Washington.

d. The Joint Forum should be reconstituted as an operational arm of the FSF.

e. The IMF and the World Bank should take the work of the Forum more seriously, and should be prepared increasingly to organize their own assessment programmes and technical assistance work in the light of priorities debated and agreed at the FSF. The Fund needs now to make a decision on where it goes next on FSAPs. The logical forum in which such a decision should be reached is the FSF itself.

f. Stronger linkages should be established between the regular FSF work on vulnerabilities, and the financial stability assessment in individual countries. At present, the nexus between these two sets of initiatives is not at all clear. There is little evidence that individual national central banks and regulators take account of the vulnerabilities work in their own assessments. There is far too much 'not invented here' in this area. There is also too little co-ordination with the IMF's Global Financial Stability Report. Greater coherence and consolidation in this area would be beneficial.

There will still be those who argue that incremental change along these lines is inadequate to the task, and press the case for a stronger central authority. Such an authority would be able to instruct the standard-setters to make changes, and indeed might take on the task of ensuring that existing standards and codes are properly implemented and enforced. It may also be possible to use it as the authority to give unchallenged legitimacy to the accounting and audit standard-setters, and in due course to actuarial standards. At this point, we continue to see little likelihood of international agreement on a stronger central body, but incremental change to the Financial Stability Forum would allow further movement in the future, if the case were to be made out.

Responding to new or changing financial entities

A related point is that the system has not proved flexible enough to respond quickly to changing types of financial activity conducted through new channels of intermediation. The sectoral structure, combined with the dominance of regulators from developed markets, makes it difficult to do so. A number of new phenomena now require an appropriate regulatory response.

The Need for Reform

Islamic finance

Islamic banking was not discussed by the Basel Committee until very recently, even though it has been growing rapidly and the regulatory system needs significant adaptation to cope with it. The Islamic Financial Services Board has done a good job in producing guidance for Islamic institutions on how they can accommodate themselves to international regulatory norms. But it is wrong that the Basel Committee and IAIS draw up standards first and consider the implications for Islamic finance later. The IFSB could be an observer at the Basel Committee, and at the Technical Committees of IAIS and IOSCO.

Investment banks

The highly diversified investment banking groups have long posed a difficult challenge to regulators. Since they are not headed by a commercial bank, they have not been subject to consolidated supervision on the traditional model. Yet their very rapid growth and present size indicates that they play as significant a role in global markets as any major bank.

The SEC, however, the obvious candidate to take on the consolidated supervision responsibility, was for long highly reluctant to do so. It argued that it was not appropriate to imply that any public support might be available in the event of trouble, and that, in any event, their balance sheets could be wound down without the risk of systemic collapse or collateral damage. Other regulators were not persuaded by these arguments.

Supervisors in Europe, where close to a half of their investment banking business was located, were particularly concerned by the lack of consolidated supervision, given the size and highly complex nature of their structures, and welcomed the Financial Groups Directive which required a form of consolidated supervision to be implemented. It is important now that the SEC implements that responsibility, and does so in a collaborative manner. There are signs that it is now prepared to do so. The investment banks have been categorized as Consolidated Supervised Entities.

Hedge funds

Hedge funds pose a novel set of problems to financial regulators. The sudden and dramatic collapse of Long Term Capital Management in 1998 put them on the agenda of regulators in all the major financial centres. The existing system was clearly not designed with them in mind, and it has proved difficult to reach a consensus on how, if at all, they should be regulated.

Why has the problem been so difficult to address? What, if anything, should be done?

All discussions of hedge funds begin with the observation that there is no convenient definition of the phenomenon. The essential characteristics of a hedge fund are that it is an unregulated vehicle (see below for some exceptions to this), which typically invests on behalf of individuals who may be its owners, high net worth investors, foundations or more recently investing institutions like pension funds or insurance companies. The funds are not normally open to retail investors (but see below), are characteristically opaque – most are privately owned and unquoted – and charge based on performance. A typical hedge fund charging structure involves a fee of 2 per cent of assets under management, together with 20 per cent of the gains on the fund, perhaps above a hurdle rate related to the interest rate on treasury bills. Hedge funds are typically seeking alpha, in other words non-diversifiable market outperformance, and often provide an opportunity to pursue investment strategies which are uncorrelated with other indices.

Hedge funds operate a wide range of strategies, including global macro funds, long/short equity funds which hold a balance of long and short positions, event-driven funds, emerging market funds, commodity funds and a wide variety of arbitrage funds, seeking to exploit mis-pricing or pricing anomalies between different asset classes.

In view of the major definitional problem, it is not possible to give a firm point estimate for the size of the hedge fund sector worldwide, but in 2007 most estimates converged around $1.4 trillion.[1] What is certain is that the volume of assets under management has grown very rapidly in recent years, and that growth looks set to continue. The largest concentrations of hedge fund managers are found in New York, Connecticut and London. The funds themselves are, however, more normally domiciled in offshore centres such as the Cayman Islands, the British Virgin Islands and Bermuda, largely for tax reasons.

As the sector began to grow rapidly during the 1990s, regulators in the major financial centres were content to sit by. As long as the funds were not marketing themselves to retail investors, were investing on behalf of individuals and institutions who could afford to lose their money, and did not engage in abusive market practices, there seemed little reason for either banking or securities regulators to take a close interest. The collapse of Long Term Capital Management changed all that. The reasons for the collapse have been well described elsewhere.[2]

In the event, the unwinding of LTCM's positions was carried out expeditiously and with a minimum of market disruption – though lawsuits to determine where the inevitable losses would fall continued for some years. In the long run, what was more important was the assessment which regulators reached of the causes of the crisis and the measures that needed to be put in place in order to prevent a recurrence of what was seen to be a 'near death' experience for the capital markets. It is important to note that LTCM's positions were huge in the gilt market in London, in the Danish mortgage market and elsewhere, in addition to its large positions in New York. Its failure, therefore, was an international issue.

Nonetheless, and inevitably, US regulators took the lead in initial assessments of the crisis and its implications. The President's Working Group, including the Federal Reserve, the SEC and the CFTC, as well as the US Treasury, reviewed the implications in the winter of

1998/9. That consideration was followed by the establishment of a Working Group by the Financial Stability Forum in early 1999. That group was invited to consider the implications of the growth of hedge funds, focusing principally on the implications of the leverage which those funds were able to achieve for the world's financial system, and to propose potential regulatory responses. It reported in the spring of 2000.[3] Broadly, its analysis followed the lines of that of the President's Working Group eighteen months earlier. The principal conclusions were that it was not hedge funds per se which posed a threat to the financial system, but their ability to gain excessive leverage, whose scale was not properly understood by the counterparties who are providing it. The report argued for greater disclosure by the largest hedge funds. It recommended new practices for the providers of leverage to funds, and better disclosures between funds and their counterparties, albeit not public disclosure. And there was a range of recommendations designed to improve the 'plumbing' of the financial system, which had shown itself to be vulnerable during the LTCM collapse. There were also recommendations targeted at hedge funds themselves, to strengthen their risk management procedures.

These recommendations were broadly accepted by the international financial community at the time, albeit with varying degrees of enthusiasm. They were reconfirmed in the 2007 review, ordered by the G7. Most have been implemented. Nonetheless, some politicians, notably in continental Europe but sometimes also in the US, have argued for more intrusive regulation of the funds. To understand the arguments better, and to identify any further regulatory steps that may be justified, it is helpful to adopt a taxonomy which separates five dimensions (albeit there are linkages between them):

1. Systemic risk
2. Leverage and prudential regulation
3. Transparency and market abuse
4. Retail investors
5. Shareholder activism.

Some politicians would add a sixth issue: taxation, but that is outside the scope of this book.

Systemic risk
Many central banks and regulators have, in their financial stability reviews, drawn attention to the risks for the financial system created by the rise and rise of unregulated hedge funds, often citing the LTCM case as a cautionary tale. It is notable, however, that many other hedge funds (some of them, like Amaranth, very large) have been wound down and liquidated without collateral damage to other market participants. Overall it would seem that, in the last decade, financial markets have not been more prone to systemic turbulence than before.

Indeed, others argue that hedge funds have, on the whole, been a force for financial stability rather than the reverse. In a discussion of the case for regulating hedge funds Danielsson, Taylor and Zigrand argue that 'the trading behaviour of hedge funds can improve market efficiency, prices and consumer choice. Furthermore, hedge funds may help in alleviating financial crisis. For example, in a crisis, when regulations compel banks to withdraw from risky investments in order to remain compliant with the minimum risk weighted capital regulations, unregulated hedge funds had no such limitations and were therefore in a position to provide liquidity when most needed.'[4]

Nonetheless, the authorities should clearly not ignore hedge funds, and the New York Fed and the Financial Services Authority have for some time engaged in a regular dialogue with the major funds, in an attempt to identify emerging systemic problems. The question at issue is whether the scale of hedge funds and the character of their activities justifies direct regulation in the interests of maintaining financial stability. Danielsson et al believe that there is a case, but that it is limited to the introduction of standing arrangements for crisis resolution, which can be implemented through an obligation on the prime brokers to collaborate with regulators in the event of a collapse. It is likely that the mechanism they propose would, in practice, come into effect in any event without the need for additional legislation. In our view, the systemic risk arguments related to hedge funds create the justification for enhanced surveillance by the regulatory authorities and central banks, rather than for direct regulation of the funds themselves. It may well be that the very existence of new patterns of risk distribution will cause markets to react differently to shocks than in the past, but it is impossible to predict precisely how or why.

Leverage and prudential regulation

The most important lesson of LTCM was that market counterparties, typically the investment banks, were providing a high degree of leverage to the fund without a full picture of the extent of its borrowings. As a result, the Basel Committee and IOSCO promulgated sets of 'sound practices' in the provision of liquidity and leverage to hedge funds, and recommended that banking supervisors around the world should police those sound practices.

But is that indirect regulation, via credit providers, sufficiently effective? Would it not be preferable to impose direct prudential controls on the funds themselves?

As to the first question, it would appear that leverage has been contained through this indirect mechanism. From time to time, however, there have been signs of declining quality of communication and of increasing leverage. This behaviour is consistent with that observed elsewhere in financial markets: the positive impact of a cautionary tale diminishes over time as animal spirits, and perhaps greed, begin to reassert themselves. There is also a collective action problem in cases where everyone agrees risk has risen, but it is a brave bank which is the first to lead by tightening or at least sticking to credit standards. It is therefore essential for supervisors to include this area in their oversight of regulated firms. No new powers are necessary in order to make that surveillance effective.

Furthermore, there are considerable difficulties inherent in the notion of direct prudential regulation of hedge funds. Indeed it may well be impossible to do so. How would an appropriate capital charge be calculated? Were a banking type regime to be followed, it is not clear that the impact would be significant. One survey has calculated that almost all hedge funds would meet a basic Basel minimum charge already.[5] Furthermore, it is not evident that a banking based approach would be helpful from the point of view of financial stability. Where hedge funds do have high leverage it is usually a result of a loss of capital created by market losses. To require funds to restore their capital base in these circumstances would create further forced sales of assets and accentuate market turbulence. In those circumstances hedge funds might not perform the positive functions which they have done in recent years, in acting as countercyclical investors and providers of liquidity at difficult times. For these reasons, most prudential regulators have reached the view that a direct imposition of such controls on hedge funds should not be recommended. We agree.

Transparency and market abuse

Hedge funds are certainly less transparent than are regulated intermediaries. They are not less transparent than other direct investors. It is important to recall that most regulation bites on intermediaries of one kind or another, where both the intermediary and the original investors see advantage in transparency from an investor protection perspective. In the case of hedge funds, investors are willing to invest through a less transparent vehicle and have not asked for the protection which mandated disclosure would give them. Regulators would need a clear public interest case for imposing such transparency. To do so would undoubtedly limit the funds' freedom, and reduce their effectiveness. That is the underlying reason why funds themselves have resisted mandated disclosure of positions. (Mandated disclosure of leverage is not necessary if the indirect regulation of leverage, described above, is effective.)

It is important to note, however, that hedge funds are subject to a variety of disclosure requirements, just as other investors are. If they cross one of the control thresholds in relation to an individual company, they are obliged to disclose those positions. Furthermore, prohibitions on the use of insider information apply to regulated and unregulated firms alike, and some high profile cases have been taken against hedge funds for abuse of information obtained in relation to corporate transactions. So it is wrong to think that hedge funds are 'unregulated' in that sense. Overall, therefore, the case for hedge fund-specific disclosure requirements seems difficult to make out.

Retail investors

Up to now, most hedge funds have not wished to market themselves to the retail sector. The cost of fund acquisition is high, the cost of communicating to a large number of investors regularly is higher, and the funds have not wanted to trigger the regulatory interventions which would undoubtedly follow were they to market themselves to unsophisticated investors. While securities and investment regulators can afford to be relaxed about the position of sophisticated high net worth investors, the person on the street requires greater protection from potentially unscrupulous intermediaries.

These arguments suggest that hedge funds should remain the province of 'consenting adults in private'. On the other hand, with some exceptions, hedge funds have delivered better returns over a long period than conventional investment vehicles. Is there not a case in equity, therefore, for finding a way of making these investment strategies available to smaller investors, who are otherwise disadvantaged by their exclusion from the market?

Over the last few years, regulators in a number of countries have reached the view that they should find a way of opening up the market to the retail sector. For the most part, they have adapted the regulatory regime for unit trusts (mutual funds) to allow individuals access to 'funds of funds' products, which reduce the risk of excessive exposure to an individual trading strategy. The European collective investment regulations are sufficiently flexible to allow this to be done. The extent to which retail investors will take advantage of these opportunities, and to which hedge funds themselves will wish to do so, remains to be seen. But no new legislation is required to allow such a market to develop.

Shareholder activism

More recently, a new dimension of the hedge fund debate has opened up, initially in Germany, but now elsewhere, too. Franz Müntefering, the German Vice-Chancellor, famously characterized hedge funds (and private equity funds) as 'locusts', landing on the foliage of corporate Germany and stripping it of its tastiest fruits.

Underlying this hostile language is a serious debate

about the benefits of shareholder activism, and particularly of private capital interfacing with publicly quoted companies. This debate, though, goes far wider than hedge funds or private equity (see below) and is essentially about the nature of contemporary capitalism. Trade unions and others argue that hedge funds and private equity firms are focused on short term gains and asset stripping and cost cutting, which results in the loss of jobs and damages the vitality of the corporate sector in the long run.[6] On the other hand, the funds themselves argue that their main impact is to stimulate sleepy corporate management to better stewardship of the assets under their control, and that companies which have been taken over by private interests have typically outperformed their publicly quoted peers. This debate is beyond the scope of this book (though we observe that those who support shareholder activism of this kind appear to be getting the better of the argument).

There are other, stronger arguments made about the activities of hedge funds. Two stand out:

- that on occasion hedge funds have seemed to act in concert with each other, contrary to the provisions of takeover codes, and
- that they have used techniques, such as open letters to management, recommending a break-up, which may themselves amount to insider information, if they are known in the market beforehand, and that some of these interventions (which have observably moved prices) have been shared with other investors beforehand.

These are serious charges, and regulators of takeovers should wish to pursue them actively. But, while actionable proof may be difficult to find, regulators have the powers necessary to pursue abusive practices of this kind, where they find them.

Our conclusion is, therefore, that the explosive growth of hedge funds has certainly created a strong argument for enhanced surveillance of the sector by regulators, from a stability perspective. To be effective, that surveillance should be as international in character as are the funds themselves. It could usefully be co-ordinated by the Financial Stability Forum, which should establish a standing group to monitor hedge funds and other leveraged institutions, which ought to include large private equity funds. In inviting the FSF to revisit its early work (which has now been done twice) G7 Finance Ministers have already recognized that there is a continuing role for the FSF, and that it is best placed to bring together the different perspectives and types of expertise needed. It would be a short step to formalize that oversight by establishing a standing group. That should include regulators from some offshore centres in which the funds themselves are domiciled, which would have the added benefit of encouraging those regulators to accept some responsibility for the funds they are pleased to accept into their jurisdiction.

Private equity

Many of the regulatory issues which arise in relation to hedge funds apply similarly to the private equity industry. The market has grown very rapidly in recent years. In the UK, the volume of new private equity funds raised in 2006 was approximately the same as the new capital raised through IPOs. On both sides of the Atlantic household name companies have passed into private equity ownership, raising concerns among the workforce and politicians.

The major issue of whether the economic impact of the growth of private equity is beneficial or not is outside the scope of this book. Industry spokesmen emphasize the positive effect on corporate profitability, productivity, growth and employment. Trade unions, in particular, focus on the secretive nature of the funds, on what they see as their asset stripping approach and argue that jobs are lost, or wages reduced, as a result of many of their transactions. The very high rewards available to the managers of private equity funds have undoubtedly fuelled this concern. Trade unions and politicians, particularly in the European Parliament, have argued for 'more regulation' of the industry, though the precise nature of that regulation is not always clear. In some cases, the argument focuses on the need for changes to the tax regime to reduce the apparent advantages available now to private equity, and to 'level the playing field' with public capital. It is also arguable that if the concern is really about very high earnings as such, the proper place to address them is through the income and capital gains tax regimes.

The current regulatory environment for private equity differs considerably from country to country. In particular, there is a difference of approach between the US and the European Union, and particularly the UK. In the US, there is no tailored regulatory regime for private equity funds. They are, of course, subject to the SEC's market regulation regime as are any investors. They are also covered by US money laundering rules. But there is no distinct category of SEC authorization which covers their activities.

The position is different in the UK. When the FSA was established a category of 'venture capital firm' was identified, with a particular set of relatively light obligations attaching to it. In addition, as in the US, market practice rules and anti-money laundering regulations similarly apply. The identification of a separate category, however, has altered the nature of the relationship between the regulator and the regulated. Consistent with its risk-based approach the FSA has identified a small group of private equity funds as 'high impact' firms with which it therefore maintains a close and continuous relationship, largely from the perspective of market surveillance and the maintenance of financial stability. The industry has, by and large, welcomed that approach.

The FSA carried out a review in 2006 of the industry and its impact. The headline conclusion was positive: 'We believe that the private equity market is an increasingly important component of a dynamic and efficient capital market. Private equity offers a compelling business model with significant potential to enhance the efficiency of companies both in terms of their operations and their financial structure'.[7]

But the review identified a number of potential risks: excessive leverage; the impact on public markets (in other words the possibility that price formation in public markets could become less robust as more and more companies are taken private); market abuse; conflicts of interest within firms leading to investor detriment; market access (the question of whether it is possible to identify a method for retail investors to gain access to the higher returns earned by the private equity industry); and opacity. This latter point has been picked up by the industry itself, which established in 2007 a working group to identify the opportunities for improvements in the disclosure and transparency of private equity funds.

These European regulatory arrangements will be amended somewhat under the new Market in Financial Instruments Directive (MiFID), but their character does not fundamentally change.

Is this regime appropriate? In our view it is, and the US could with benefit adopt a similar approach. The private equity industry is now so large that it is not realistic for regulators to ignore its potential impact on the market. On the other hand, it is not clear that the activities of private equity funds raise issues which are so different in character as to justify a radically different approach. As with hedge funds, private equity firms are borrowing from sophisticated investors on the one side, and are themselves shareholders – two groups which are not offered significant protections under the regulatory regimes now in place,. So the main regulatory issue is one related to financial stability and market integrity, which argues for surveillance and good information flows, rather than capital requirements or new conduct of business rules.

However, the issue of the impact on public markets of a significant shift from public shareholdings to private ownership is potentially very significant. Were a private equity to come to be the dominant form of ownership of major corporations, many aspects of investor protection and market regulation would need to be rethought. We have not reached that point yet, but we could usefully prepare for it.

Cross-border exchanges and securities markets

Within the EU, cross-border exchanges such as Euronext or OMX are subject to broadly the same rules in the various countries in which they operate, so that the regulators of each national marketplace can in principle collaborate without too much difficulty as a college of regulators. But how will a Stock Exchange owned in a third country be regulated? Whose rules will apply? The UK government rushed through emergency legislation in an attempt to prevent the creeping arrival of US regulation in London in the event of a takeover of the London Stock Exchange. This demonstrated that the existing system had not yet adapted to this possibility. With the creation of transatlantic ownership links, as with NYSE-Euronext, this issue has to be addressed.

In the short term each country can stick to its own regime. However, if such mergers are to move beyond shared trading technology to create real unified markets, then fundamental changes are needed to handle regimes which have structural differences. Faced with this new market reality, the regulators on both sides of the Atlantic have expressed the intention to make an equally fundamental change of approach. (In fact the UK has long followed this approach, though the SEC has in the past rejected it.) Instead of requiring foreign players to play by domestic rules, applying extraterritorially where necessary, the plan is to switch to mutual recognition of each other's regimes for foreign issuers or investors. Mutual recognition normally takes place on the basis of broadly similar standards, even if differently delivered, as happens in banking regulation. It is too early to say how this process will unfold in the exchange or broader securities field where there has generally been greater reluctance to agree standards, partly arising from major differences over the way in which retail investors are best protected. It will sharpen the debate about where and how standards are set and with what legitimacy, and break down yet further the notion that regulation is a purely national (or EU) matter.

Offshore financial centres

The Financial Stability Forum 'blacklist' of offshore financial centres, introduced in 2000 but withdrawn in 2006, had a significant impact on them. The outraged reaction demonstrated that the criticisms were near the bone, especially in the case of centres in the 'bad' and 'ugly' categories. The work by the IMF and the World Bank under the FSAP also served to highlight weaknesses in some centres, and to promote an upgrading of standards. It seems likely, therefore, though this is hard to prove, that offshore centre regulation is now somewhat more effective than it used to be, and closer to the standards obtaining in onshore markets. But in our view there remain vulnerabilities. Information exchange with offshore centres is still more difficult than elsewhere. Quite apart from the tax leakage, there are difficulties in tracking risk transference between sectors, when it passes through offshore jurisdictions, and the Financial Action Task Force has drawn attention to weaknesses in our defences against money laundering. There are continued suspicions, too, about insider dealing which passes through these centres. The London market is full of rumours of a 'Monaco ring' operating in Monte Carlo, although these rumours are always hard to pin down.

In our view, therefore, in spite of the improvements made in recent years, remain a concern. We think a continued focus on their regulatory standards and practices is well justified. To that end, we recommend three approaches:

1. Continued pressure from the IMF and the World Bank to improve standards. Some FSAP reports identified weaknesses in compliance with international standards and codes. On a targeted basis the Fund and the Bank should follow up those specific recommendations to identify whether the gaps have been filled. Where they have not, they should publicize the fact.
2. The more important offshore centres should be brought more closely into the work of the key international regulators. There could, for example, be an offshore representative on the Basel Committee,

charged with promoting liaison between Basel and the offshore centres themselves, and indeed with encouraging non-compliant centres to come into line. The same could be done with the technical committees of the IAIS and IOSCO.

3. As with hedge funds and private equity, there is a case for a continued oversight function, located within the Financial Stability Forum. That could build on the useful work carried out by the earlier grouping, albeit there might now be a case for operating in a somewhat less confrontational manner. That group would be charged with producing occasional reports on the application of standards and codes across offshore jurisdictions, reports which could be submitted to G7 Finance Ministers.

The role of the international financial institutions

The FSAP has been a major and time-consuming exercise, with some benefits, albeit perhaps not commensurate with the costs. The evaluation reports described in Chapter 3 highlight the advantages and disadvantages.

Since the assessments have now been completed once for almost all countries though notably not in the case of the US or China, and gaps and weaknesses identified, it would be reasonable now to focus the programme more tightly on jurisdictions with significant problems. A regular programme of major across-the-board reviews would be hard to justify. On the other hand, abandoning the exercise entirely would be a mistake because the

FSAPs have value in maintaining ongoing best practice and ensuring as a counterweight to political pressure that after initial reforms supervisory independence is sustained. The regulatory groups themselves, who rely on voluntary participation by states, cannot be expected to take on an enforcement role. The prospect of a visit by an IMF team can serve to create an impetus for reform, especially in countries where financial regulators struggle to secure the resources they need to be effective.

The IMF should also co-ordinate its FSAP work more closely with the FSF. The Fund could put forward a work programme for discussion at the Forum, to ensure that there is input from regulators who deal directly with problem countries. Hitherto, the Fund has set its own priorities without consultation. Priorities could be determined according to (a) the extent of significant problems, (b) their systemic importance in the global economy, (c) recent changes to the regime and (d) a request from the supervisor in question.

Further reform in Europe

The creation of a single financial market across the European Union is a highly ambitious programme. As we explain above, much progress has been made in harmonizing rules and regulations across the continent, and in removing some of the protectionist barriers erected by individual member states. But, as we also explained, the progress has been hampered by a lack of clarity about the end point and the underlying objectives of the programme. For instance, the logic that the benefits for end users under the single financial market programme may only come with a reduction in costs and in employment in financial services may not be generally understood or accepted. There will need to be individual losers for the efficiency gains to be achieved, including within the regulatory community.

Some have seen the project as essentially about removing barriers to cross-border transactions, especially in the wholesale area, creating the opportunities for greater competition between financial firms and financial centres. Perhaps naturally, with a highly competitive financial sector already, and Europe's leading financial centre, the UK has been associated with that strand of thinking. Also, because of its continued absence from the Eurozone, policymakers in the UK have been less concerned about retail competition where currency risk creates a continued natural barrier, whatever the regulatory arrangements. Other countries have been motivated rather differently. They are very anxious about the impact of the single currency on their retail markets. And, if they are potentially major importers of financial services, they will typically prefer to see standardized regulation to ensure there is no incentive for such domestic institutions as they still have to move business elsewhere. At the same time, while large firms can see that standardized rules could bring cross-border advantages, small firms simply see the changes needed to bring this about as all cost and no benefit.

The political salience of these arguments is high. The differences of view are not qualitatively different from those which apply in other areas of the European Single market. But there are some special characteristics in the financial sector. Financial business, and firms, can move more quickly and easily from country to country than can manufacturers. In wholesale markets, in particular, the concept of capacity is extremely elastic. It is possible for a 'winner takes all' phenomenon to develop quickly, as has been demonstrated in some sectors of the wholesale markets in London. There is also, perhaps, more political sensitivity about the location of financial centres which are seen, like national airlines, as symbols of national virility. The contortions which some financial groups have got into in trying to locate themselves in jurisdictions where there this is political resistance to 'delocalization', as the French would have it, have been striking. Politicians are not yet reconciled to the idea that a national financial services centre may fade away as most municipal or regional stock exchanges have done. There is also a related fear that the relocation of financial providers may have a broader impact on the rest of economy, in that other businesses may find it more difficult to attract capital as a result. It is hard to prove that this is so, although it is striking that a much larger percentage of venture capital and private equity has been invested in the UK rather than other European countries. On the whole, however, this is attributed to other factors, notably to the less regulated product and labour markets in the UK which have proved attractive to overseas investors, and to favourable tax treatment. Nonetheless, the view that finance is somehow 'special', and that its location can influence other parts of the economy, is strongly felt by European politicians.

These factors explain why Europe has reached the current position. The single market can hardly be said to be complete, and there are some crucial areas in which no European regulatory framework has yet been established. Clearing and settlement is a case in point. There are other gaps in retail markets. Yet there is little appetite for further legislation, after the wave of directives in the last decade (though the case for a directive on clearing and settlement because of the critical role this plays in the overall soundness and efficiency of markets will remain strong if the market fails to reach an acceptable outcome. Commissioner McCreevy has made his own view on that point clear, responding with sensitivity to views strongly expressed in the markets and in national capitals, but willing to legislate if the market fails to deliver.)

As far as the structure of regulation is concerned, what has been put in place since the Lamfalussy Report is highly complex (see Chart 5). The committees, sub-committees and working groups continue to proliferate. It is hard to avoid the conclusion that the negotiation costs of the Lamfalussy system are extremely high. Furthermore, even where legislation has been implemented, the way it is put into effect in each jurisdiction varies greatly. There is a long list of reasons for this, deliberate political fudges in the Level 1 legislation, lack of clarity about what is expected at Level 2, desire to keep idiosyncratic national arrangements where not explicitly banned, variations in reporting frameworks, differences in supervisory culture and techniques, decisions only when there is consensus at Level 3 – and so on. Lying behind this is a further question about whether there should be different requirements for large cross-border groups, and for national, retail firms in relation to which the cost of change might exceed the cost of further standardization. This debate highlights the lack of clarity about the aims of the project. And there is little discussion as to whether single market imperatives are consistent with risk reduction, which tends to be the preoccupation of regulators. So we need to ask whether we have reached a stable resting place, or whether other changes, whether in legislation or regulatory structure, will be needed if the single financial market is to reach its full potential and be as efficient as if it were a national market.

There is no available consensus on the answer to that question, though it is clear that few people are content with the position as it stands. Wymeersch[8] notes that a number of proposals for reform have been made, including the creation of an optional additional jurisdiction for pan-European firms. Wymeersch himself argues for gradual change, leading to a position in which there are a small number of financial centres acting as home supervisors of all the systemically important firms, with some agreement between countries on burden-sharing in the event of a bail-out.

In the UK, and perhaps a few other countries, the dominant strand of opinion would be hostile in principle to any further standardization and certainly to centralization. Most politicians, and indeed many market participants in London, would oppose any institutional change and, in particular, reject the creation of a single European regulator, seen by some as cutting through the above thicket of problems at a stroke. While the FSA is exposed to its fair share of criticism on individual measures, and is regularly accused on 'gold plating' Commission directives, this criticism rapidly fades if the spectre of a single regulator, based in Frankfurt, Brussels or Paris, is raised. The FSA then becomes a national treasure which must be preserved at all costs. And it is not only in the UK where there is resistance to the creation of new European authorities. The French and Dutch referendums on the European Constitution demonstrated that, for now, support for new European initiatives cannot be taken for granted even in countries in which the tradition of support for the EU is strong. With increased efficiency at the EU level comes loss of some local jobs. Where would these cuts fall?

On the other hand, as Wymeersch acknowledges, there are influential voices arguing for change. Firms are trying to construct pan-European business models which, they argue, will reduce costs and thereby create a more efficient market for both owners and users of capital. Exchanges and infrastructure providers continue to try to merge cross-border. They point out that they are obstructed from doing so because of significant differences between the member states, and that the existing directive framework allows those differences to persist. They increasingly argue that, unless European regulation is genuinely standardized, on a maximum harmonization model, they cannot secure the full benefits of the single financial market. Some argue too, notably

Deutsche Bank, one of the firms which has made strongest efforts to create a pan-European entity, that the logic of the single market points ultimately to the creation of a single financial regulator. There are voices in the European Parliament arguing the same point. Their arguments are felt to be particularly strong in the case of the Eurozone countries. There are those who suggest there are potential lacunae in the defences against financial instability in the Eurozone and go on to argue that this too argues for more centralization. If a large pan-European institution establishes itself with headquarters in a smaller member state, will the financial institutions of that member state be capable of providing the kind of lender of last resort support which might be necessary in a crisis? Indeed, with the specialization of functions between different centres it is not clear that subsidiaries, even if legally independent, could be independently viable. What would the role of the European Central Bank be in these circumstances? Is there a need for a single institution in the Eurozone, whether the ECB or a newly created regulatory body, with an overall financial stability remit?

In the area of crisis management there are clearly issues to resolve in reconciling clashing national rules governing the dividing up of a cross-border institution's assets after a failure, and arrangements are needed to prevent individual supervisors freezing assets in their jurisdiction in the rush to maximize their share of a failing group's assets. It would as a minimum be sensible to think through in advance the different options for distributing fiscal responsibility for solvency support to a cross-border group. Governments, and it is they, not central banks, who are responsible for the public funds spent in solvency support, cannot agree in advance to fixed formulae, but they will need to have a range of options ready to facilitate decisions which will need to be made in a matter of hours.

At present, as we say, political appetite for further change, whether legislative or structural, is strictly limited. In the short term, attention should focus on regulatory co-operation, where there is much scope for improvement, on pan-European training of regulators, on peer-reviews to monitor national compliance, and on bringing the three Lamfalussy committees together. But we should nonetheless ask what would make sense in the longer term. In particular, is there a robust case for a single European financial regulator? Could we reach the position where it is no longer sufficient for national regulators to rely mutually on each other? And in any case, there is no turning back from the radical change which has been already launched.

More heat than light has been generated by this debate in recent years. There is considerable uncertainty about what is precisely meant by a single regulator. Are we talking about rule-making or supervision or both? Are we talking about all sectors or only some? If we mean a body which is capable of generating pan-European legislation in financial markets, then we have a single regulator already, in the form of DG Markt in the Commission. Perhaps DG Markt could and should be strengthened so as better to create coherent pan-EU rules. One could also, at the limit, imagine a separate federal-like entity created to oversee Europe's financial markets and draft new uniform laws, but that would strike at the heart of the Commission's monopoly on proposing legislation and on the member states' role in transposing it, and would be an extremely fundamental change in the European legislative architecture.

Another definition of a single financial regulator which has been advanced is that of an all-powerful authority which would oversee the implementation and enforcement of European directives in all member states. This also looks implausible. For the foreseeable future, the legal structures in individual member states differ so much that transposition and implementation are bound to vary in form and, even if national regulations were to be identical, the manner of enforcement in the court systems of individual countries can be very different. Just as there is no equivalent to US federal law, so there is no equivalent to federal courts. Again, a new institution in this category looks most unlikely politically.

But is there an argument for a different type of single financial regulatory body, operating in the territory between EU legislation, on the one hand, and national day-to-day supervision and enforcement on the other?

This is the territory currently occupied by the three Committees of supervisors – CESR, CEBS, and CEIOPS – and their constellations of sub-committees and working groups. While European directives are typically somewhat more detailed than, say, corresponding domestic legislation in the United Kingdom, they nonetheless require considerable articulation by regulators at what has come to be known as Level 3. At the moment, that articulation is carried out on a collaborative basis between sovereign domestic regulators. Would it be preferable to replace this network solution with a single authority charged with the creation where needed, of pan-European rule books and uniform supervisory practices, which would then be implemented and enforced by authorities in individual member states? In our view, the answer to this question is yes, and we believe Europe will need to move towards the creation of a single financial regulator, in this specific sense, if the single financial market is to achieve its objectives as we understand them.

It is evident that not every rule can or need be identical, but the new authority could be mandated to apply a number of principles. In particular, it would need to decide when rules and supervisory practices needed to be identical in form and application or when just in outcome so as to maintain a level playing field, or whether they needed to be identical at all. In determining where a rule should be identical in all jurisdictions it should decide whether this would promote or inhibit competition. For a discussion of some of these issues see the article by Ferran and Green 'Are the Lamfalussy Regulatory Networks working successfully?'[9]

It may be that these issues cannot be resolved without a further fundamental review of what the single market in financial services is intended to achieve, perhaps along the lines of Lamfalussy's own review, and of whether the existing legislative framework, once implemented, is found to be fundamentally fit for purpose. If it emerges, as we expect, that more rather than less standardization is needed, but in carefully defined circumstances, then the new authority's mandate can make this clear.

The existing legislative framework, enhanced by recent and prospective legal developments in relation to lead supervision, provides significant scope for effective co-operation between regulators so the mandate should be to produce the effect of unitary regulatory arrangements and decision-making. Where firm or market arrangements are or could be identical across jurisdictions, there should be a presumption of identical regulatory treatment from which divergence needs to be justified. This authority would also set the basis for the day-to-day supervision of cross-border groups and, whenever possible, the regulators of a group should voluntarily exercise their separate sovereign powers in an identical way so as to produce the effect of a single regulator for that group.

A number of ideas has been put forward for putting in place structures which deal with the challenge of prudential supervision of cross-border groups. One example is that advanced by Stefan Ingves, Governor of the Swedish Central Bank, who has suggested a gradual process whereby a centralized institution first co-ordinates the risk assessment of cross-border groups and gives advice to national supervisors mediating where conflicts arose. If that works then this body could take on additional powers, hence mitigating the cost of an extra layer of supervision.[10]

Would that regulator, whether just for regulations or also for prudential supervision, be a Eurozone body, or a European Union body? That is less clear. There is greater pressure, and incentive for the creation of a single regulator in the Eurozone than there is outside it. Perhaps the Eurogroup will elect to move in this direction sooner, creating a difficult dilemma for the UK government and for the governments of those other countries which remain outside the single currency. The legislative logic is that any new body should be a Union wide construction and of course financial groups do not stick to Eurozone boundaries (nor, indeed, EU boundaries), but the practical outcome is much less certain.

There is also the question as to whether such a body could be put in place without new legislation, by the individual regulators acting in concert. In practice, that would mean boosting the secretariats of the Lamfalussy Committees, to allow more work to be done centrally, on behalf of all countries, with less committee intermediation. That would be likely to be more efficient, and it may be that the basis of trust between authorities, which has been built up over a period within the Lamfalussy structure, will soon create the conditions in which a more centralized approach could work more effectively.

Finally, there is the question of whether Europe needs one centralized regulatory body, or three. Our view on this will be clear from our arguments above on regulatory structure. Given the increasing integration of the marketplace, and the blurring of lines between the sectors, it would make little sense to create a European Banking Authority, a European Securities Authority and a European Insurance and Pensions Authority. So the creation of a new European financial services authority should go hand in hand with further reform in individual member states. We will not manage to create a more rational and market-friendly regulatory structure within Europe without rationalization both centrally and locally. Even then a solution which works purely in pan-EU terms will need to work within the global regulatory environment in which financial markets operate. Any new European Authority will need very close co-ordination with both the European Central Bank and the central banks of individual member states which play host to systemically significant banks.

Conclusion: new leadership required

Financial markets change rapidly. The last few years have seen particularly dramatic shifts in both the character and location of transactions. Credit derivatives, scarcely understood a decade ago, are now a huge part of the system. New intermediaries have proliferated.

Inevitably regulators struggle to keep up. That is not surprising, but they should not lag far behind. At present, the structures within which they work make it hard for them to address emerging issues: they were devised in a simpler time, when a bank was a bank and a broker a broker.

Regulators are also – again perhaps inevitably – conservative folk (with a small c). That is as it should be. They have a tendency to cling to outdated institutions and methods of working. So for change to occur, leadership is needed. The body best placed to exert leadership is the G7 finance ministers. Unfortunately, they often have bigger fish to fry: trade imbalances, fiscal problems etc. So a final constructive change would be for the G7 to establish a ministerial group on financial regulation, to oversee the FSF, the IFIs, and the regulatory group-ings, and keep the system under review. Had such a group met, and commissioned urgent work from the FSF in the summer of 2007, that could usefully have raised confidence at a nervous time.

It would be better for this to be done before the arrangements we have described find themselves tested to the limit by the emergence of a crisis which demon-strated just how far the reality of global markets has changed from the time when the existing architecture of regulation was designed.

Afterword

The bulk of this book was drafted in the first half of 2007. While the events of the second half have not come as a surprise, arising as they have out of the evolving structure of global financial intermediation we describe in Chapter 1, both their rapidity and the ever widening ramifications pose a challenge for us in reviewing in January 2008 whether the conclusions we drew in the late summer of 2007 still hold.

For the most part we think they do. Nothing that has happened undermines the case for integrating yet further the regulation on a cross-border and cross-sectoral basis of both firms and markets. Indeed governments have already started down the route we advocate. The G7 has already directly charged the Financial Stability Forum and its constituent agencies with analysing the causes of the current market turmoil and with making recommendations to address them. These will emerge during the course of 2008. We expect the role of the FSF to be further strengthened and governments to be readier than in the past to implement its recommendations.

The role played by sovereign wealth funds in providing capital to the leading global financial firms has also provided a sharp reminder of the need to amend more generally the global institutional structures for regulation to provide proper representation of those whose interests are at stake, and the opportunity should also be taken to deal with shortcomings in other features of governance. The need to bring China, in particular, into full membership of the key groups has become more urgent.

We also highlight the inadequate attention given in recent years to the links between real economy and financial developments. The credit crisis has underscored the point and we expect the IMF and others to devote much more attention to those relationships in their economic surveillance in future. Central banks have been reminded that credit may need quite as much attention as money if their aims of both financial and monetary stability are to be met.

We can also now see that regulators have not paid enough attention to liquidity supervision, while engaged on the Basel solvency regulation project. Banks have always gone out of business when they could not pay their liabilities when they fell due, however strong their net worth. This distortion of supervisory focus has had a cost and it is welcome that previously discredited models such as liquidity mismatch ladders are to be re-examined urgently as supervisory tools.

Recent market developments, as well as competitive pressures, have concentrated minds on the need to produce globalized standards in the sphere of financial reporting. The very rapid moves towards truly global accounting standards, and the more forthcoming attitude of the SEC, have been a welcome surprise. They provide the opportunity to reform the global governance arrangements for both accounting and auditing standards.

It is too early to say whether radical changes in regulation are needed for hedge funds, private equity or rating agencies, though the latter have suffered significant reputational damage and need to work hard to restore confidence in their independence and integrity. It may be that heightened public awareness of the economic reality of the risks involved in the kinds of intermediation involved will of itself bring about adequate market-led adjustments to behaviour. Certainly, many market participants have become aware that to entrust funds to institutions whose structures are opaque, on the basis of credit assessments that are inadequately understood, is a riskier business than they thought.

Clearly, the debate about the structure of supervision at the national level is set to continue in all the major economies, with changes under lively debate almost everywhere. Nothing has emerged to detract from our premise that an integrated, cross-sectoral approach remains vital. Nor do we believe that the UK trilateral arrangements for crisis management are fundamentally unsound. Three different functions and sets of policy objectives exist: financial supervision, monetary policy and the management of financial markets, and access to the public purse, and any system of decision-making has to give adequate weight to each of these three elements. The UK government may, however, be wise to clarify the leadership role of the Treasury in a crisis.

The suggestion that the insolvency arrangements for banking in the UK need to be changed serves as a healthy reminder that the unsatisfactory insolvency arrangements for financial firms operating cross-border, particularly complex ones, remain a critical weakness in the overall financial architecture, albeit happily hitherto untested on any material scale. The crisis management issue is being taken up with renewed seriousness within the EU, though it remains to be seen whether the political conflicts of interest that exist will make it possible to put in place robust arrangements to resolve a cross-border crisis. And in any case this will still need addressing at the global level by the FSF, since any serious crisis affecting firms in the EU will have implications for the wider world.

Another issue which continues to receive close study at the EU level, but which is also of global significance is 'supervisory convergence'. In our view the term 'convergence' remains an unhelpful one. What is needed is to determine in what circumstances regulation needs to be *identical in form* and implementation so as to secure economy and efficiency for firms, their users and regulators alike, to determine where it needs merely to be *identical in outcome* to secure competitive equality, and to determine where it is enough for there to be some kind of, sufficiently effective to give to others the confidence to rely on it, yet flexible enough to permit innovation and to maintain the capacity to respond to the changing requirements of the users whose needs regulation is ultimately designed to serve.

Events since the summer of 2007 have increased awareness of the importance of global financial regulation; we hope that the volume will aid understanding of the structure and limitations of that regulation as it has developed so far.

References

1 The Objectives of International Financial Regulation

1 Globalization and Capital Markets. Maurice Obstfeld and Alan Taylor. National Bureau of Economic Research. Working Paper 8846, March 2002
2 *Global Finance at Risk. The Case for International Regulation.* John Eatwell and Lance Taylor. Polity Press. May 2000
3 Interim Report of the Committee on Capital Markets Regulation. November 2006. www.capmkts.org
4 *The Age of Turbulence.* Alan Greenspan. Penguin. New York and London 2007
5 The Economic Rationale for Financial Regulation. David Llewellyn. FSA Occasional Paper No. 1. April 1999
6 *Finance for Growth: Policy Choices in a Volatile World.* World Bank Publications. May 2001
7 Crises Now and Then: What Lessons from the Last Era of Globalization. Barry Eichengreen and Michael Bordo.

References

National Bureau of Economic Research. Working Paper 8716. January 2002.

8 *Lombard Street – A Description of the Money Market.* Walter Bagehot. London 1873

9 Memorandum of Understanding between the Bank of England, HM Treasury and the FSA. 1997. www.fsa.gov.uk

10 *Rethinking Bank Regulation: Till Angels Govern.* James Barth, Gerald Caprio, Ross Levine. Cambridge University Press 2005

11 Defining and Achieving Financial Stability. Bill Allen, Geoffrey Wood. LSE Financial Market Group. Paper 160. April 2005

12 Financial Stability Review 1996 – www.bankofengland. co.uk

13 Some New Directions for Financial Stability. Charles Goodhart. Per Jacobsson Lecture 2004. www.bis.org

14 Central Banks and Financial Stability: A Survey. Sander Osterloo and Jakob de Haan. *Journal of Financial Stability* (1) 2004

15 Anatomy of Financial Crisis. Rick Mishkin. National Bureau of Economics Research Working Paper No. 3934. 1991

16 Two Cheers for Financial Stability. Howard Davies. Group of Thirty. Washington. 2006

17 Sustaining New York's and the US's Global Financial Services Leadership. McKinsey and Co for the City of New York. January 2007.

18 www.wto.org

19 Evaluating Better Regulation: Building the System. Graham Mather and Frank Vibert. European Policy Forum. September 2006. City of London Research Series

2 The Current International Regulatory System: Theory and Practice

1 www.bis.org/bcbs

2 www.Basel2implementation.com

3 www.iif.com

4 www.fdic.gov

5 Guidelines for Developing Effective Deposit Insurance Systems. Financial Stability Forum. September 2001. www.fsforum.org

6 www.iadi.org

7 www.bis.org/cpss

8 www.fatf-gafi.org

9 Initiatives by the BCBS, IAIS and IOSCO to combat money laundering and the financing of terrorism. Joint Forum. June 2003. www.vis.org/bcbs/jointforum.htm

10 www.iosco.org

11 The Structure of International Markets Regulation. Chapter 13, p. 455 in *Financial Markets and Exchange Law*. Oxford University Press. March 2007

12 Securities Regulation – An International Perspective. Jane Diplock, Chair, New Zealand Securities Commission. 17 October 2006. www.sec.com.gov.nz

13 www.world-exchanges.org

14 www.iaisweb.org

15 Reinsurance and International Financial Markets. Group of Thirty. Washington 2006. www.group30.org

16 The IAIS Common Structure for the Assessment of Insurer Solvency. February 2007

17 www.thepensionsregulator.gov.uk

18 www.iopsweb.org

References

19 www.bis.org/bcbs/jointforum

20 www.pcaobus.org

21 www.ifac.org

22 www.ipiob.org

23 www.ifiar.org

24 www.iasb.org

25 www.oecd.org. OECD Principles of Corporate Governance. OECD 2004

26 *Islamic Finance: The Regulatory Challenge.* Edited by Simon Archer and Rifaat Ahmed Abdel Karim. John Wiley. 2007

27 www.ifsb.org

28 Supervisory Implications of Islamic Banking: A Supervisor's Perspective. Toby Fiennes. In *Islamic Finance: The Regulatory Challenge.* Edited by Simon Archer and Rifaat Ahmed Abdel Karim. John Wiley. 2007

29 Islamic Finance and Financial Policy and Stability: an Institutional Perspective. Andrew Sheng. Islamic Financial Services Board Inaugural Lecture 26 March 2007

30 Report on Offshore Centres, IMF 2000. www.international monetaryfund.com

31 Report of the Working Group on Offshore Financial Centres. Financial Stability Forum 2000. www.fsf.org

32 Quoted in 'Places in the Sun'. *The Economist.* 22 February 2007

33 www.taxjustice.net

34 www.fatf.gafi.com

35 FSF announces a new process to promote further improvements in offshore financial centres. 11 March 2005. www.fsf.org

3 The International Financial Institutions and their Role in Financial Regulation

1   Report to G7 Ministers and Governors by Hans Tietmeyer on International Co-operation and Co-ordination in the area of financial market supervision and surveillance. 11 February 1999. www.fsforum.org
2   Report on the Evaluation of the Financial Sector Assessment Program. IMF Independent Evaluation Office. January 2006. www.imf.org
3   Financial Sector Assessment Program: Key Findings and Recommendations. 2006. www.worldbank.org
4   *Rethinking Bank Regulation: Till Angels Govern*. James Barth, Gerald Caprio, Ross Levine. Cambridge University Press. 2005

4 The European Union: A Special Case

1   www.europa.eu/internal_market/top_layer/index_24_ en.htm is the source of most basic information on the EU single market in financial services.
2   Reordering the Marketplace: Competition Politics in European Finance. Daniel Mugge. *JCMS* 2006 Volume 44, Number 5
3   Financial Services Action Plan 1999–2005. COM (1999) 0232
4   Green Paper on Financial Services Policy (2005–10). Paper prepared for City EU Advisory Group. Corporation of London July 2005. p. 30
5   Financial Integration Report. ECB. March 2007

References

6 *MiFiD – an opportunity to profit.* Graham Bishop. Logica 2006

7 Communication from the Commission to the Council and the European Parliament – Modernizing Company Law and Enhancing Corporate Governance in the European Union – A Plan to Move Forward. COM (2003) 0284

8 Green Paper on Retail Financial Services in the Single Market. European Commission. COM (2007) 226

9 Final Report of the Committee of Wise Men on the Regulation of European Securities Markets. European Commission. 2001

10 www.cesr-eu.org

11 Stockholm European Council Conclusions, Annex 1, March 2001

12 www.c-ebs.org

13 www.ceiops.org

14 Impact Assessment Guidelines for EU Level 3 Committees. CESR/07-089, CEBS 2007 28, CEIOPS-3L3-07/07

15 Supervising Financial Services in an Integrated European Single Market: A Discussion Paper. HM Treasury / FSA / Bank of England. January 2005

16 Burden Sharing in a Banking Crisis in Europe. Goodhart and Schoenmaker. *Economic Review* 2/2006

17 Financial Supervision in Europe: Do we need a New Architecture? Cahier Comte Boël No. 12: February 2006

18 Towards a New Structure for EU Financial Supervision. Speyer and Walter. Deutsche Bank Research. August 2007

19 On the lead supervisor model and the future of financial supervision in the EU. June 2005. www.efr.be

References

20 The Future of Financial Regulation and Supervision in Europe. Eddy Wymeersch. *Common Market Law Review*. January 2005

5 Regulatory Structures in Individual Countries

1 *How Countries Supervise their Banks, Insurers and Securities Markets*. Freshfields Bruckhaus Deringer. Central Bank Publications 2007

2 *The Age of Turbulence*. Alan Greenspan. Penguin. New York and London 2007

3 Introduction to the Blue Sky Laws. Richard Alvarez and Mark Astarita. www.seclaw.com

4 Financial Regulation: Industry Changes Prompt Need to Reconsider US Regulatory Structure. Report to Chairman, Committee on Banking, Housing, and Urban Affairs, US Senate. US Government Accountability Office. October 2004

5 *The View from Number 11: Memoirs of a Tory Radical*. Nigel Lawson, Bantam Press 1992

6 *Twin Peaks: A Regulatory Structure for the New Century*. Michael Taylor. Centre for the Study of Financial Innovation. 1995

7 See, for example, *The Prudence of Gordon Brown*. William Keegan, John Wiley 2003

8 Global Financial Centres Index March 2007. Z/Yen Group for the Corporation of London. www.cityoflondon.gov.uk

9 Financial System Inquiry Final Report (Chair Mr Stan Wallis). Canberra. March 1997

References

6 The Debate on Regulatory Structure

1 The Rationale for a Single National Regulator. Clive Briault. Occasional Paper 2. May 1999. www.fsa.gov.uk
2 *Financial Regulation.* Goodhart, Hartmann, Llewellyn, Rojas-Suarez and Welshrod. Routledge. London 1996
3 *Twin Peaks: A Regulatory Structure for the New Century.* Michael Taylor. Centre for the Study of Financial Innovation. 1995
4 Report of the Royal Commission into HIH Insurance. Canberra. 16 April 2003
5 The Pursuit of Financial Stability. E. A. J. George. 1994. Bank of England. www.bankofengland.co.uk
6 Central Banking and Bank Supervision in the United States. Chairman Ben Bernanke. American Social Sciences Association Annual Meeting. Chicago 5 January 2007. www.federalreserve.gov
7 Rethinking Inflation Targeting and Central Bank Independence. Willem Buiter. London School of Economics. 26 October 2006. www.lse.ac.uk
8 Independence and Accountability. Briault, Haldane and King. Bank of England Working Paper No. 49. www.bankofengland.co.uk
9 Institutional Structure of Financial Regulation and Supervision: The Basic Issues. David Llewellyn. In *Aligning Supervisory Structures with Country Needs.* Ed. Carmichael, Fleming and Llewellyn. World Bank Institute. Washington 2004
10 Does Regulatory Governance Matter for Financial System Stability: An Empirical Analysis. Das, Quintyn and Chenard. Bank of Canada. 2004. www.bankofcanada.ca

References

11 The Fear of Freedom: Politicians and the Independence and Accountability of Financial Sector Supervisors. Marc Quintyn, Sylvia Ramirez and Michael Taylor. IMF Working Paper. Washington. February 2007

12 Sustaining New York's and the US's Global Financial Services Leadership. McKinsey and Co for the City of New York. January 2007

7 The Need for Reform

1 www.hedgefundresearch.com

2 *Investing Money: The Story of Long Term Capital Management and the Legends Behind It.* Nicholas Dunbar. John Wiley. 1999

3 Report of the Working Group on HLIs. April 2000. www.fsforum.org

4 *Highwaymen or Heroes: Should Hedge Funds be Regulated?* Danielsson, Taylor and Zigrand. Journal of Financial Stability 2005

5 Do Hedge Funds have enough Capital? Gupta and Liang. *Journal of Financial Economics* 77 (2005)

6 Aneurin Bevan Memorial Lecture. John Monks, General Secretary of the European Trade Union Confederation. 14 November 2006

7 Private Equity: A Discussion of Risk and Regulatory Engagement. DP 06/6 Financial Services Authority. www.fsa.gov.uk

8 The Future of Financial Regulation and Supervision in Europe. Eddy Wymeersch. *Common Market Law Review.* January 2005

References

9 Are the Lamfalussy Regulatory Networks working successfully? Eilis Ferran and David Green. European Financial Forum. August 2007

10 Regulatory Challenges of Cross-Border Banking – Possible Ways Forward. Stefan Ingves, Governor, Sveriges Riksbank. *BIS Review* 73/2007

Index

Index

Index

Index

Index

Index

Index

Index

Index

Index

Index

Index

Index

Index